TIM BROOKE-TAYLOR'S
GOLF BAG

TIM BROOKE-TAYLOR'S
GOLF BAG

Illustrated by Borin Van Loon

Stanley Paul
London Sydney Auckland Johannesburg

Stanley Paul and Co. Ltd.

An imprint of Century Hutchinson Ltd

Brookmount House, 62–65 Chandos Place
Covent Garden, London WC2N 4NW

Century Hutchinson Australia (Pty) Ltd
88–91 Albion Street, Surry Hills, NSW 2010

Century Hutchinson New Zealand Limited
191 Archers Road, PO Box 40–086, Glenfield, Auckland 10

Century Hutchinson South Africa (Pty) Ltd
PO Box 337, Bergvlei 2012, South Africa

First published 1988
Copyright © Tim Brooke-Taylor 1988

Phototypeset by Input Typesetting Ltd, London
Printed and bound in Great Britain by
Butler and Tanner Ltd, Frome and London

British Library Cataloguing in Publication Data
Brooke-Taylor, Tim
   Tim Brooke-Taylor's golf bag.
   1. Golf – Humour
   I. Title
   796.352′0207

ISBN 0–09–173702–8

CONTENTS

Marker's Signature _____   Handicap ____
Player's Signature _____   NET SCORE ____

LOCAL RULES

1. **Out of Bounds**
   All other books adjoining book on bookshelf.

2. **Folded over Pages**
   Folded over page corners may be folded back. Players are responsible for removing their bookmarks after reading.

3. **Unreadable Pages**
   Players may obtain relief from torn or mutilated pages by reading a page of similar length from another book without loss or penalty.

4. **Marmalade**
   Where two or more pages have been stuck together with marmalade the book may be lifted and cleaned provided the reader doesn't turn over sixteen pages and pretend he's nearly finished.

5. **Flies and wasps**
   The book may be used to swat flies and wasps that are annoying the reader without penalty provided it isn't returned to the library with the bits still on it.

INTRODUCTION

How To Play This Book

If there is one word in golf that I dread it is 'good'. This is a 'good' hole. It's a 'good' test of golf. The course is in 'good' condition. He's a 'good' golfer. This needs a 'good' drive.

Substitute the word good with 'impossible' and you've more or less got the idea.

A 'good' hole means a 400-yard plus hole uphill against the wind. Out of bounds left and right and your drive must be at least 200 yards to clear the water. It is also within view of the secretary's office.

'Wentworth is a good test of golf' means even the pros find it difficult. The high handicapper finds it akin to going to the dentist's and having all his teeth out. Yet he'll still pay over £30 for the green fees. Now the East course is not a 'good' course, and there's an awful danger you might actually enjoy playing on it. Likewise, the Old Course at St Andrews is a 'good' test, especially in the wind and the rain. Whereas the Eden course may be aptly named because it is paradise to play but it is not a 'good' test. Swinley Forest must be a really bad course because it is probably the most enjoyable course I have played in Britain. What is more it is, horror of horrors, a flattering course.

The greens are in 'good' condition – they are lightning fast and totally unreadable. This needs a 'good' five iron – it's all you've got.

So I hope you don't find this a 'good' read. I hope you find it an enjoyable read. Some of you may wish to play all eighteen chapters at once and then maybe again after lunch. If you're thinking of a quick nine for the time being, may I suggest the brewer's loop – chapters 1, 3, 7, 9, 11, 14, 15, 17 and 18. Now remember, nice and easy, don't rush it, and don't lift your head until you've reached the bottom of the page.

Have a nice round!

CHAPTER ONE

GOLFING AROUND THE WORLD

GOLF AN OPENING HOLE

MY putt came to a halt. Then, I swear to you, it started to trickle uphill. My partner had an explanation. 'Remember,' he said, 'all putts go from the mountain to the sea. It may look uphill but it is in fact downhill. Of course the nap of the grass is against you, but this is compensated for by the platform of the green.'

From that moment on I developed the yips – a nervous twitch in the putting stroke which increases in ferocity the closer the putt is to the hole.

This book was written during the winter of 1987/88 in an attempt to exorcise the yips. The theory was that if I were to fill my head with every little-known golfing fact and figure there would be absolutely no room left for anything else, like doubt for example.

Has it worked? Well, I sit here in April with a broken arm, not able to put it to the test. It has been suggested that I broke my arm on purpose to put off the evil day; for I still wake up in the middle of the night in a muck sweat having dreamt of a six-inch putt to win the Open, only to see the ball sail out of bounds as a result of a huge yip.

I don't think I broke my arm on purpose. I'm not conscious of doing so. It was just the result of some inaccurate skiing. But I'm not certain. Sometimes death seems preferable to the yips. So a broken arm is really nothing.

I have tried the Bernhard Langer 'Yipmeister' but even the built-in aversion therapy (40,000 volts through the handle if the stroke isn't firm and resolute) failed to 'cure' me. In fact I grew quite fond of the electric shocks.

I am grateful too, for another German firm, Yippenunterdenschaft who had read about my condition in the Christmas edition of *The Lancet*. In theory their Technoputting system should work. There is nothing intrinsically wrong with the use of laser technology; and the incorporation of micro computers built into the head of the club not only marks a major breakthrough in design but also falls within the rules of golf. Unfortunately it still requires an actual human being to hit the ball. In this case, a human being with the yips.

The AWAK early warning system could also be useful enabling me to see the line of a putt from about three thousand miles away. And that, after

all, is the position I'd like to be in when I make most of my putts – three thousand miles away.

The search to cure my golf has given me a lot of material for this book. Since I started playing the game, golf equipment has improved enormously. The ball itself has changed out of all recognition. Gone is the 'ball in paper' with its foul smelling innards of gutta percha and its eggshell-like cover. Now we have the Dunlop 65 GTi with overhead camshaft, and my personal favourite, the Wilson Super XD diesel turbo, the 'talking' ball. The Wilson is now refined to the point where it not only talks but can hold quite a meaningful discussion with a player in fourteen different languages.

BALL: Well how are we today, then? Ready to beat the living daylights out of me are you?
ME: Yes, yes I think so.
BALL: Good, I like a man who knows what he wants. See 'Horizon' last night did you?
ME: No, I was watching the film on ITV.
BALL: Pity, I'd have been interested in your opinion Tim. You don't mind if I call you Tim, do you?
ME: Well actually I'd rather . . .
BALL: Good. It was about AIDS of course . . .
ME: Of course . . .
BALL: Seemed a bit alarmist if you ask me, of course I know what you're going to say, can you be too alarmist about something as serious as that, well I mean it's all very well . . .
ME: Look I'm . . .
BALL: Oh I'm sorry Tim, you want to start don't you. You know me, once I'm off there's no stopping me. Alright here we go. Now remember take the clubhead straight back. Good. Complete the backswing and down through the . . . Bloody Hell!

There are some who argue that the modern game has become too technical and suggest a back-to-basics, no-nonsense, wholemeal, bran-and-yoghurt sort of golf. When they say, 'this shot requires a wood' they mean this shot

requires a reconstituted-waste-products-to-look-and-perform - like - wood - but - avoiding - any - further - destruction - of - the - world's - rainforests. These brown rice golfers aren't in favour of measured courses and the blight they cause on the natural landscape at all, but instead advocate what they call Golfocross – a mixture of golf, orienteering, and point-to-point. Unfortunately the pro-hunting lobby objects to this sport as it upsets the breeding habits of foxes and huntsmen. Recent Golfocross meetings have been ruined by the release of packs of hounds trained to sniff out and devour the golfballs; and if necessary tear the golfers themselves limb from limb. An excellent spectator sport but in this case a shocking waste of human resources.

NEW GOLF

To most golfers, however, natural golf is an anathema, the more complicated and technical the better as far as they are concerned.

The Courses

The greatest stars in golf today are not the players but the architects. They are sadists to a man. They take a piece of land. They mark out a course and wait for it to grow. They then allow a few golfers to play on it, study their rounds, and make the necessary alterations. If say on the first tee the player finds himself with the glorious prospect of a wide open fairway, downhill, wind behind and with the contours such that two reasonably hit shots will naturally tunnel the ball onto an inviting green – then it must be changed. Some will just reverse the hole; uphill against the wind. Others will place a bunker or a ditch or, in extreme cases, a lake, right across the fairway or the natural line. New American courses make an increasing feature of water, so much so there is very little land left, and all of that slopes towards the water. The consequent skill enhancement of continually playing out of water has led to an entirely new sport; Aqua Golf.

*Aqua Golf: the latest craze from America. The entire eighteen holes are played underwater.
(Players whose ball lands on temporarily dry land may obtain relief under the 'casual land' rule and drop their ball into the nearest puddle without the loss of a stroke)*

Designer Bunkers

Another new development has been the arrival of the designer bunker. Unfortunately not all these bunkers have been designed by artists conversant with the rules of golf. The Lacoste course in Florida boasts the prettiest bunker groupings I have ever seen, but as they have been constructed at the back of every tee they rarely come into play. Similarly the distinctive Ralph Lauren 'polo playing' bunkers on the Spiro Agnew course in South Carolina have been so placed that no-one will ever land in them, for otherwise the club hacker might easily ruin the perfect lines.

NEW COMPETITIONS

Some of the new style competitions that have caught on in the last few years include

(a) *The five-ball greensomes*
All players drive five balls from the tee. They then play their four worst drives as second shots, their three worst second shots as their third shots and so on until they are left with one ball. If they hole all second shots they get eight points. If they hole the single ball in one it is two points. If however they fail to hole the single ball first time then they forfeit two points for every extra shot.

(b) *The eighteen-hole dash*

Everyone drives off together and the first to finish wins. Players must play out each hole, but no strokes are counted. Players must not interfere with other players' balls – or for that matter with other players. Here we see the players under starter's orders. The official is making sure that no-one oversteps the starting mark

[11]

(c) *Hide and seek*

Ray Floyd takes part in the 1986 US PGA Hide and Seek Competition

(d) *Blindfold golf*
Each player is blindfolded. Caddies may shout instructions. This is a very slow moving and exceedingly dangerous form of golf. Not recommended.

(e) *The Brockenhurst Scramble*
Whereas in the Sunningdale Scramble players play the first, fifth, twelfth, fourteenth, seventeenth and eighteenth holes in order, in this case the complete reverse is true. In the matchplay version of the Brockenhurst, players must play the ninth but not the fourth, and the sixth but not the eighth. The eleventh cannot be played unless the eighteenth and the fourteenth are played in preference to the tenth and the third, in which case the first, seventh and twenty-sixth must be played eleven times each.

N.B. For the Brockenhurst Scramble the square root of seven-sixteenths of current playing handicap is allowed.

(f) *One-legged golf*
The author demonstrates

(g) *Yorkshire rules*

If there is a Yorkshireman playing he must win. If there are two or more Yorkshiremen competing then they are deemed to have come equal first.

THE SPREAD OF GOLF

Once an international airport was the status symbol of an emerging nation. Nowadays it is the golf course. Where once zebra and wildebeest mingled by the waterhole, now Lee Trevino and ministers of finance play over it. Arab states are justly proud of their 18-rig courses where billions of barrels of oil are bet just on the back nine. Sometimes even more for the 'press'. But is the world being overgolfed? The sight of millions of Japanese in tartan trousers and pompon hats with hip flasks full of genuine Samurai Scotch Whisky only being able to play on driving ranges is worrying. But that's not really our problem, is it?

CELEBRITY TOURNEYS

The Bob Hope Classic and Bing Crosby events are now well established in the golfing calendar. But as the search for sponsors continues, the ranks of lower-echelon celebrities are bound to be plundered and called to take their turn.

Among those events presently being considered for the celebrity circuit are:

The Sooty Classic
The Ali from EastEnders Pro-am
The Sid Little Charity Golf Tournament
The Reg Varney One-Star Championship
The Postman Pat Champion of Champions
The WPC Phelps from Crimewatch UK World Matchplay
The Girl Who Drapes Herself Over the Prizes in 3–2–1 Round Robin Event

THE WORLD OF GOLF TODAY

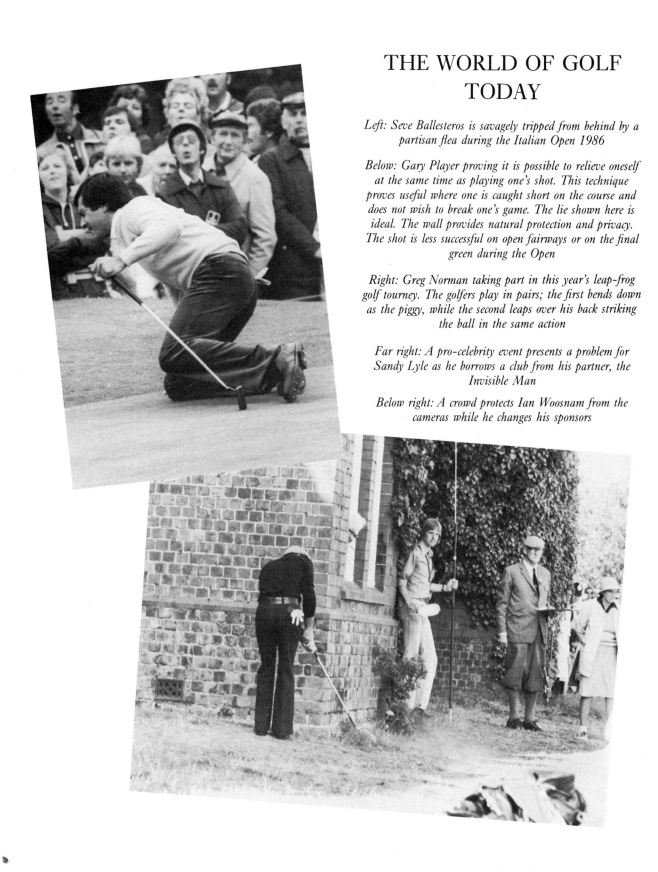

Left: Seve Ballesteros is savagely tripped from behind by a partisan flea during the Italian Open 1986

Below: Gary Player proving it is possible to relieve oneself at the same time as playing one's shot. This technique proves useful where one is caught short on the course and does not wish to break one's game. The lie shown here is ideal. The wall provides natural protection and privacy. The shot is less successful on open fairways or on the final green during the Open

Right: Greg Norman taking part in this year's leap-frog golf tourney. The golfers play in pairs; the first bends down as the piggy, while the second leaps over his back striking the ball in the same action

Far right: A pro-celebrity event presents a problem for Sandy Lyle as he borrows a club from his partner, the Invisible Man

Below right: A crowd protects Ian Woosnam from the cameras while he changes his sponsors

Morris golfing. The British and European Morris dancers prepare to take on the USA in the Morris Dancers Golf Cup. The rules are very simple; the players play out each hole as normal but before proceeding they must May Dance round the flag. The game has still to catch the public's imagination

CIA men discreetly guarding Gerald Ford during the Bob Hope Classic

*The SAS Golfing Society
(Motto: 'Who Dares Wins, 4 and 3')*

*Diet plays an important part in many players' lives.
Here Jack Nicklaus shows how a banana diet has
drastically affected his figure*

Before

After

CHAPTER TWO

THE GOLFER'S HALL OF FAME

Any hall of fame must, perforce, be a personal one, its portals filled with those players who have given one a special thrill, or impressed in some unique way.

This is my hall of fame and I make no apologies for including names that may be unfamiliar or who would not find a place in others' golfing galleries. Indeed, many will perhaps not have heard of a single name I list. But to me they are the champions of the sport, and it's my list, so there!

RUFUS PUMPKIN

Early twentieth-century pioneer of the golf buggy, his steam-powered 'commodious wagonette for golfers' bore more resemblance to a primitive traction engine than to a modern golf cart. Its precipitous approach down the fairway belching clouds of sooty black smoke regularly disturbed the play of fellow golfers, while the steady emission of hot coals and clinkers set light to no fewer than three golf courses during the vehicle's brief history.

Rufus Pumpkin's 'commodious wagonette for golfers'. With a gross payload of twenty-three tons it was capable of carrying even the heaviest club bag. Seen here on the tenth at Turnberry with its owner

HORATIO GROUT

Opened the first golf driving range in Kentucky in 1926 charging 50 cents for half an hour, balls and club free. Unable to find a net large enough to collect the shots he instead adopted the novel idea of employing an army of local youngsters whom he trained to stand fifty yards down the 'fairway', baseball gloves at the ready, with the instruction that they were to catch any drive that might come flying towards them. The range proved to be an immediate and resounding success, though not with the parents of the boys.

SIR PERCY 'TWITCHER' SANDRINGHAM

Former club president at the Oddfellows Club, Little Beeslea. An outspoken and forceful player whose chronic slice was no obstacle to a good score on his own course. The Oddfellows eighteen are unique as they are the only known case of a custom-built golf course. 'Twitcher' employed an architect who marked out eighteen tees on open ground and measured Twitcher's drives. As the round continued the slice became more pronounced, so that by the eighteenth it was virtually a 90-degree arc. Trent Smith, the architect, then systematically altered the Oddfellows course according to Twitcher's measurements. As life president and sole benefactor of the club Sir Percy was in the happy position of finding his plans passed unanimously – one for, none against. Twitcher, not surprisingly, won the first monthly medal on the new course with a remarkable 58 stableford points. The runner-up had 36 points, the highest of his career by far, because he, like Sir Percy, was a chronic slicer. Within weeks Sir Percy's handicap was down to single figures. Just as rumblings were beginning to be heard from the other members, Twitcher developed an equally impressive 'hook' which he countered by insisting the course be played in reverse. For several years the new course at the Oddfellows Club retained a sort of novelty

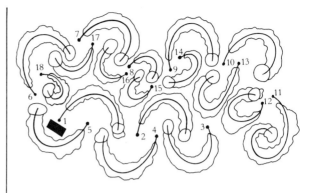

The new course at the Oddfellows Club showing a typical round by Sir Percy

value, with players travelling from all over the country to play the near impossible holes. Sadly though, just as Twitcher was rising up through the club's ranks sweeping every shield and medal competition before him, he was to find himself the victim of cruel fate. For one day, as if by magic, after watching the final round of the Open on television, he found it quite impossible to hit the ball anything but dead straight. No longer was he invincible on his own course, being able to play it neither forward nor in reverse, and with falling interest the club took the inevitable step of reverting to the original layout.

C. T. GREGSON

Sparky North Country professional who in 1946 led the Welsh Amateur Open by using a set of club heads to which he had ingeniously attached a small explosive charge. The effect of this was evident from the very first tee when Gregson strode up to his ball, addressed it with composure, swung his club with gentle ease, and was greeted with a bang, a blinding thunderflash and the sight of the ball speeding away up the fairway like a mini rocket, covering an astonishing 450 yards before the first bounce. Unfortunately Gregson was quite unable to predict the extra distance his 'supercharged' club would achieve and he quite regularly overdrove the green by anything up to two or three hundred yards. Eventually the affair literally backfired on him when he trod on one of his own fully primed club heads in error and found himself unceremoniously deposited in the branches of a nearby tree. The Gregson club was outlawed by the R & A immediately after the tournament, although it did go on to give several years' excellent service with the Royal Navy coastal command.

MRS EMELIA WUTHERINGTON

Suffragette and chairwoman of the Women's Golf Association. Her particular responsibilities were to ensure the advancement and progress of the women's cause in the field of golf. She set about them with verve and gusto, protesting at many golfing events and at one stage chaining herself to the great Harry Vardon's bag before the final round of the Open. With the lock key unavailable

Commemorative trophy celebrates Mrs Emelia Wutherington throwing herself under the King's club in support of the women's golfing movement

and time pressing, Vardon's caddie volunteered to carry Emelia plus bag round the full eighteen holes on his shoulder, an offer that Vardon reluctantly accepted (R & A rules state that no more than fourteen clubs may be taken out on the course by any one player, but do not stipulate how many disenfranchised women may be carried).

LIEUTENANT-COLONEL SPOONER

Daredevil American 'stunt' golfer who flew for many years with a barnstorming circus and adopted much of the same devil-may-care philosophy towards his golf game. He would often encourage new or unsuspecting playing partners to lie on the grass, a ball balanced precariously on the end of their nose, whereupon he would take out a stout two wood and attempt to drive the ball clear from its impromptu tee. 'He's done it again!' became a common cry from the clubhouses around Spooner's native Wisconsin as another hapless victim staggered into the clubroom nursing a bleeding nose and badly bruised lip. Perhaps the Colonel's most famous stunt came during a 1928 'novelty' contest in which players were encouraged to compete for the most original round of golf. As the quaint and colourfully dressed competitors gathered on the first tee ready to perform their exotic tricks, a loud roar suddenly erupted behind them, and looking round in horror they were just able to dive for cover as Spooner burst over the horizon in a frail boxplane, one hand on the rudder while the other thrashed around frantically beneath the aircraft with a seven iron, gamely trying to tee off a nearby ball. The fact that Spooner insisted on playing out the entire round in this airborne manner says a great deal about the man's raw courage. Certainly the vision of him swooping down low over a three-foot putt with engine screeching and putter dangling feebly from outstretched hand will live forever in the memory of those lucky enough to see it.

PATRICK W. SNOAD

Legendary pioneer and golfing enthusiast who encouraged the idea of 'courseless' golf, arguing that the formal arrangement of a course only stifled the natural exuberance of the golfer and that it was better for players to plot courses according to their own whims. Setting out early Patrick would select a suitable patch of open ground and, checking first for passers-by, he would drive off into the distance, hitting each new shot as it took his fancy. Travelling in this way Patrick would traverse as much as thirty or forty miles of rough country in a day without once stopping to sink a single putt or fill in a solitary scorecard. Of course, the sight of Patrick chipping his way through some unsuspecting farmer's yard, or blasting his way out of some poor person's prize rose garden with disastrous results, is one that non-enthusiasts will debate. But for several years in the middle of the last century the Snoad approach to golf represented an exciting new challenge. A number of the chronicles Snoad wrote during these travels ('Across Wiltshire by Seven Iron', 'Compleate Golfing Travels', 'Dorsetshire Golfing Routes', 'Putting The Pennine Way') are collector's items today.

T. J. WHITWORTH

Amateur golfer regarded by many as the father of the knitted golf club head cover. It was Whitworth who in 1932 knitted a first crude prototype (now on permanent display at the Museum of Knitted Golf Club Head Covers, St Andrews) that was to take the designated title Whitworth 1. Twenty years later came the turning point with the release of Whitworth 472, the first head cover to have a dangly knitted pompon attached. Just eight years after that came the roll-out ceremony for Whitworth 672, the first knitted head cover to go into commercial production.

—————— GREAT GOLFING INVENTIONS ——————

To this hall of fame must be added a special selection dedicated to the great inventors. For golf has in its time contributed to many of our great discoveries, and no archive is complete without reference to the great strides in science that the game has engendered.

ARCHIMEDES

Perpetual Golf Hole

Although none of his later discoveries depended upon the game of golf, there is evidence that Archimedes did cut his teeth as an inventor thanks to golf. Working through his papers we are able to see crude reference to what has become known as the Archimedian Perpetual Golf Hole. It appears to work accordingly. The hole is situated

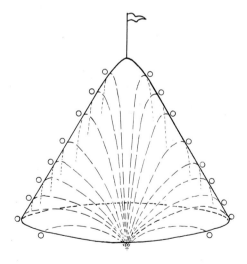

The Archimedian Perpetual Golf Hole. The gradient is constant throughout. It is calculated to be just sufficient to ensure no ball may come to rest on the slope

at the top of a perfectly symmetrical mound. The gradient is sufficient to prevent any ball remaining on the slope. Any shot played up the slope will naturally fall away from the hole and slip back to the base. Only a shot played with great speed directly up the slope will reach the hole. And this shot will travel far too fast to stop. The golfer is left in a state of perpetual motion.

Archimedes' Perpetual Golf Hole

$$X = \left[\frac{Y^2 + \left(\dfrac{q}{p} \middle/ \dfrac{Q}{Zrmb} \right)^2}{96 \times \sqrt{100n \div \dfrac{P}{\pi}}} \right]^{1/3}$$

x = angle of slope required
y = rub of green
q = index of left forefinger
p = velocity of putter
z = windchill factor
r = air temperature
m = length of grass in inches
Q = number of dimples on ball
b = number of dimples on caddie's chin
n = player's birthsign

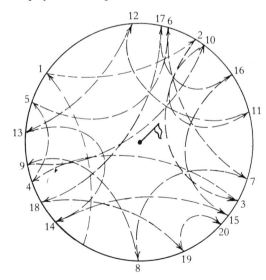

A sample of 20 shots taken at the hole by one player

RUTHERFORD

Splitting the atom

It is a little-known fact that the great scientist Ernest Rutherford chanced on his greatest achievement through a golfing accident. Playing five off the tee in a game of golf he resolved that the only way to make progress was through sheer brute force. Accordingly he took a one iron to the well teed-up ball and drove it with all his might. The effect was immediate. The lower half of the ball remained untouched on the tee, the upper half that he had topped so crudely flew a full fifty yards down the fairway: the first recorded splitting of a golf ball. At once Rutherford curtailed his round and dashed immediately to his laboratory and set to work. Six years later the atom had been split and Rutherford had achieved immortality. Alas, his golfing record is not so well documented.

ISAAC NEWTON

It is well recorded that Newton developed his understanding of the laws of gravity through watching an apple fall from a tree. What is not appreciated is that this in turn led to a number of other valuable discoveries: the multi-compound golf ball, the flat sand iron, the pro-am golfing holiday complex, and the Ben Crenshaw pro-am seat stick umbrella.

ALBERT EINSTEIN

Molecular theory

Another great scientist who took inspiration from the golf course was Albert Einstein. It was while knocking around a number of practice balls on the putting green that he became aware of the patterns these balls made. Suddenly these patterns filled him with the notion of molecular structures, and his life's work began to drop into place. Along with his putts, many of Einstein's early models were based directly on examples borrowed from the golf course.

Einstein discovers molecular structure on the putting green

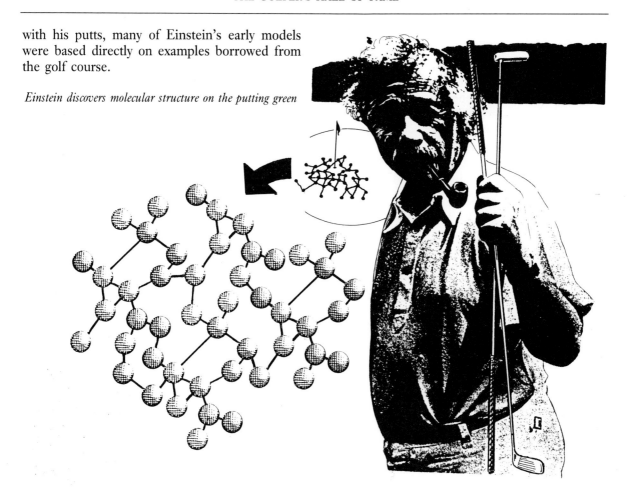

—————UNUSUAL GOLFERS—————

Finally in this hall of fame, I would like to set aside one corner for those groups whom I believe qualify for a special place in the game's history; groups who through their very obscurity deserve exposure.

The Golfing Bushmen of the Kalahari

First discovered towards the end of the nineteenth century, they represent perhaps the earliest and most primitive golfers in the world today. Living as they do in a vast desert, their game is fashioned almost completely around sand iron play. The result is a golf style that does not lend itself to the conventional course. On the odd occasion that one of their members has been encouraged to play a Western course, spectators have been alarmed to discover the Kalahari golfer deliberately driving for the bunkers and raising his warshield in jubilation every time the sand is found.

The Hell's Angels Royal & Ancient Chapter

It is unusual to find golfers who are into motorbikes, leather and Def Lepard gang bangs.

However, a small but thriving chapter has grown up in recent years, dedicated to the sport of golf. Look out for their characteristic Harley Davidson caddie cars with cow-horn handlebars. Look out too for their distinctive line in golfing knitwear – neat paisley pullovers with the words 'Motorhead' and 'Whitesnake' printed on the back in studs.

The Beastie Caddies (Rare)

Look out for torn tee-shirts, golfing trolley badge necklace, and alarming tendency to jump up and down on the side of the green, swearing at fellow golfers and rapping their scorecard down your ear.

The Dangerous Golfing Club

A radical offshoot wing of the Dangerous Sports Club. They arrange golfing tournaments where the emphasis is on danger and risk. So far they have organised: a tournament up the Colorado River in which the players attempt to play an eighteen-hole course laid out along the length of the Grand Canyon whilst shooting the rapids on an inflatable raft; a medal competition through the rainforests of the Congo Basin, from which there were no survivors; and the world's first matchplay contest between a golfer and an anaconda (match halved).

The Stanislavski Golfing Society

A society set up to apply the work of the great theatrical actor/director in a golfing context. Members of the society are encouraged to explore the reason and motive for their performance and to adopt the 'method' school of play.

THE STANISLAVSKIAN SCHOOL OF IMPROVISED GOLF

A four-day golfing workshop

RATIONALE

Golfers will be taught to extemporise their emotional understanding of the golfer set against the backcloth of the post-modernist approach to method golf. Improvisation classes will be held in which golfers are encouraged to research their characters and discuss their motivation.

PROGRAMME OF EVENTS

Discussion during the course will include:
1 Street golf
2 The role of golf in the community
3 Contemporary golf and mime (a look at movement and dance for golfers)
4 Modern experimental golf
5 Alternative golf
6 Left-wing golf and the role of golf in political fringe theatre today
7 The interpretation of golfing neo-realism

CHAPTER THREE

THE TOUGHEST COURSE I'VE EVER PLAYED

ONE of the questions that I am often asked is what is the most difficult course I have played.

It is an awkward question because so many spring to mind. I remember the back nine on the fearsome Aleutian Islands championship course: rainfall of over eight hundred inches a month, a constant shroud of mist, ninety-mile-an-hour gales, sub-zero temperatures, sea swells that could throw a sixty-foot wave across the links at any time; and a four-foot tin shed that served as the clubhouse.

Or I could cite the equally daunting Yukon Old Course, a real monster this with no hole less than two miles long and a par for the course of 7418; a course where the local rules contain a fifty-page advice leaflet on basic survival techniques; home of Endurogolf, the fast-growing sport combining the life-and-death struggle of man pitted against nature with a round of golf.

Alternatively I could select the tricky little Goose Green course, down on the Falkland Islands. A seemingly straightforward set-up but with the added complication of twelve unexploded minefields and a precariously close weapons range.

But of all the courses, one stands out as being the ultimate in the challenge it offers. I am talking about the course that has broken so many golfers' hopes, and necks: the Annapurna New Course.

Here are those eighteen holes that still send a shiver down my spine as I recall the horrors they wrought upon me when I last played the Annapurna Pro-Celebrity in 1982.

1st: 472 yards, par 92
A fine opening hole, nearly 472 yards up a near vertical scree slope. The loose gravel makes securing a foothold impossible and every shot carries with it the very real risk of starting an avalanche. The hole has absolutely no fairway at all and requires a drive to the green (a four-foot craggy outcrop) in one. Crampons essential.

2nd: 782 yards, par 237
The only way even to reach the tee is by parascending from a helicopter. The hole is reached by a nine-hundred-step rope ladder.

3rd: 613 yards, par 126
A monstrous hole, comprising a completely vertical drive played from a rocky two-inch ledge overhanging a 4000-foot-deep ravine. Caddies and players must rope up for this hole. The flag position is deceptively easy: the trick is to hit a small rocky outcrop three hundred feet above and the ball will ricochet directly into the hole.

4th: 911 yards, par 4457
Totally uncompromising. It makes the escape sequence from Indiana Jones seem like a Sunday afternoon jaunt in the car.

5th: 318 yards, par 957
Another completely vertical hole. However, there are no bunkers, which explains the surprising amount of eagles recorded.

6th: 747 yards, par 2071
This hole is completely and utterly unplayable at some times of the year. The player must swing out on a rope to hit the ball upwards in a double corkscrew vortex to carry to the only ledge 352 feet above. From here it is an equally daunting 371-yard strike to a lone cormorant's nest, from where there is a comparatively easy chip to the flag.

7th: 875 yards, par 256
Totally and utterly and completely unplayable. What golfers call a 'good' hole.

⑦

8th: 417 yards, par 820
First of the *really* difficult holes. A sheer granite slab faces the player from the narrow 3/4″ outcrop of rock to the tiny mist-shrouded flag perched on a totally inaccessible ledge 800 yards above.

⑧

9th: 992 yards, par 3
Forget it if you are even only mildly affected by vertigo. Another 'good' hole.

⑨

10th: 201 yards, par 27
On the surface an easier hole this. Unfortunately the shot requires precise footwork, perched over a 7000-foot precipice with nothing beneath to prevent certain death. Watch out for the buzzards that attack anyone who comes within fifty yards of their nests and the howling gale that can freeze a man to death in under five minutes.

⑩

11th: 347 yards, par 411
Nicknamed 'The Impossible Hole'. This is the toughest hole I have ever known. Roped to your caddie against the sheer face of the mountain, you require a manufactured 300-yard vertical slice. Many players simply concede the hole before reaching the tee. The rest concede before they even reach the course. The stroke index of 18 is absurd.

⑪

12th: 827 yards, par 4564
The hole is down at 827 yards but in fact normally plays at least two yards longer. Hence the reason for many of the misjudgments. Extreme lack of oxygen a problem after the first 150 feet.

⑫

13th: (uncharted), par (unknown)
The Lost Hole of Annapurna. So treacherous it has never been successfully climbed. In 1958 a four-ball expedition to play the north side of the hole perished on the mountainside. Their clubs were never found.

14th: 448 yards, par (on application)
Another brute. Plays a three wood to the first inaccessible ledge. Then a three iron to the next inaccessible ledge. And finally a nine iron to the totally inaccessible flag. A 'good' test of golf.

15th: 613 yards, par 741
The flag has been moved three feet since I last played the hole, which should make it a lot easier. Kendal mint cake advisable.

16th: 314 yards, par 242
Another comparatively simple hole. Most players aim to make par on this hole. An eagle is possible, especially if you hit it on the beak just as it flies past. Not a particularly 'good' hole.

17th: 579 yards, par 234,567
This hole has been likened to trying to chip the Atlantic Ocean blindfold. Jack Nicklaus took six here when he last played!

18th: 47 yards, par 56
An easy hole, complicated by being at the very top of the mountain. Any slackness on the approach is likely to be penalised by the ball plummeting to the foot of the mountain leaving you to start all over again.

CHAPTER FOUR

THE RULES OF GOLF

RULES

In previous days the rules of golf were very simple. In 1823, for instance, there were no rules. In 1811, even fewer. In 1799, less still. Yet gradually, as the game became more sophisticated and the situations in which players found themselves became more awkward, many players stopped playing golf altogether and started making rules instead. By 1903 no fewer than 6043 rules existed and the rules committee (comprising four hundred people) were adding to them at the rate of 45 a month. Indeed, during one remarkable month the rules committee actually managed to log up an incredible 246 new rules, plus 74 amendments and 321 clarifications.

It became apparent that unless something was done the game could become swamped with rules, and in 1907 a group of golfers led by Sir Horace Cutthorpe invaded the committee rooms, overthrowing the previous committee in a bloodless coup, and purged the game of 95 per cent of its rulebook.

Six months later this faction was itself deposed by the right-wing sympathisers of the previous committee under the guise of the Sons of Golfing Martyrdom, a fanatical grouping with astonishing zeal who set about inventing new rules at an unheard-of rate.

No fewer than six further revolutions followed, in each of which a new rules committee was set up and overthrown. At the end the bloodied committee rooms were in disarray. A total of 21,987 different rules had been introduced, repealed, re-introduced, overturned, re-sanctioned and finally repealed again. No fewer than 32 editions of the rule book had been published in little under eighteen months. Everyone was growing weary of the struggle.

It was therefore a relief when a coalition of all groups came together on 1 September 1912 to lay down finally the foundations of the modern rule book.

Since then there have been disagreements and discrepancies. In 1927, in a violent argument, 38 members of the rules committee were forcibly debagged in a disagreement over the preferred lie rule. In 1938 there was a nasty skirmish in which the leaders of the then rules committee were locked in a public lavatory for four days until they agreed to look again at the lost ball rule. And in 1951 the chairman of the committee was tied to a chair in a leading London fish restaurant and told that if he didn't alter the ruling on provisional balls then he would never see his sweet course again.

Of course, incidents such as these are now thankfully rare and we seldom have incidents like the notorious St Valentine's Day Massacre of 1931 when the members of the rules committee were lured to a deserted warehouse and systematically given each other's haircuts until they agreed to change rule 15B. Nowadays the rules are well established and agreed upon.

The ball is played where it lies

For practical purposes the rules of golf are comparatively simple. The most basic, and the rule upon which all others are based, is that '*the ball should be played where it lies*'.

Diehard fundamentalists still adhere strictly to this law. These 'Plymouth Brethren of golf' will do nothing to acknowledge the progress of time, and if the ball lies in the middle of the railway line with an express due any second, then that is where it shall be played and no excuses. You will see them halfway up a cliff face strapped to a rope, gamely trying to scoop the ball out of a precariously balanced puffin's nest. Or stripped to the waist in swimming trunks and snorkel, trying to extricate the ball from some icy watery grave.

However, for the rest of us with better things to do with our time than fish old bicycle frames out of quarry holes, there came into being the term 'obtain relief', which as well as the act of easing the bladder in a nearby gorse bush also came to refer to the means by which a player might finish a hole by taking penalty shots for his waywardness.

Of course, if present trends continue there is an undoubted danger that the erosion of golf's hardy image may be weakened still further as relief is obtained for ever more fanciful reasons: a bunker in the way, a butterfly on the fairway, a car backfiring six miles away. But for the time being the rules that chiefly concern us are in the Copy of Rules that most weekend golfers carry with them on the course and which condensed briefly may be stated thus: ⟶

—— RULES THAT WERE NEVER REPEALED ——

A number of unusual and interesting rules of golf have, surprisingly, never been repealed. As a variation of the normal game, arrange a competition to see how many you can break during a round. Among those still in the rule book are:

1 Besmirching the good name of Catherine of Aragon on the course is a treasonable offence.
2 The parking of a sedan chair on the putting surface is an offence, two shots or forfeit the hole.
3 Attempting to secure the release of Prussian prisoners of war on the putting green is punishable by death and/or a fine of fifty bushels of hay.
4 Fornicating with the devil: four-shot penalty.
5 Harbouring a follower of Oliver Cromwell in one's golf bag: execution and four-shot penalty.
6 Being a foreigner: forfeit the match, any match.
7 Attempting to prove the world is flat while making a putt: deportation to the colonies.
8 Having a caddie who is a witch: ducking in water.

THE RULES OF GOLF

Ball played as it lies

You must play the ball as it lies, unless the rules allow you to do otherwise. You must not knock it forward with your toe when no one is looking; or pretend to trip over and in so doing roll your ball on to a handy mound or tuft by hand. Bending down to check a ball belongs to you and surreptitiously moving it forward a few inches when everyone else's backs are turned is definitely not on. A false-bottomed golf bag that opens to drop a spare ball in a better lie is a complete no-no. Unless no one is looking.

Ball lost, out of bounds, unplayable

If you hit your ball into what you consider is an unplayable lie, you may not pick it up to check it is yours then throw it back casually on to the fairway with the cry: 'Oh look what I've done, what a silly billy, I've completely ruined that brilliant lie I had and ended up with this awful one. Oh well never mind, I suppose I'll just have to suffer the consequences.'

With one stroke penalty you may drop within a two-club length to either side or back as far as you like. You may not drop out on to your foot and drop-kick the ball 200 yards down the fairway with a cry 'Ye-es! Lineker, what a goal!'

Nor may you have a club which telescopes out to forty or fifty yards.

Relief from loose impediments

An obstruction is something erected or placed on the course but does not include fences and walls marking out of bounds. You may move natural objects not fixed or growing, e.g. stones, leaves, twigs and, on the green, dirt and sand. You may not remove trees, rivers, small mountains, or the contents of other people's pockets.

Provisional ball

If you think that your ball may be lost or out of bounds you may play a provisional ball from the original spot before going forward. If you think that your *provisional ball* may also be lost or out of bounds you may play another provisional ball. If you play more than twenty-five provisional balls at any one hole before leaving the tee then you should consider giving up the game and becoming a monk.

Casual water

Casual water is water that is not a permanent fixture on the course. It does not refer to water that goes around in casual clothes and loafers. If your ball is in, or you have to stand in, casual water or ground under repair, you get a free drop within two club lengths of the nearest margin or area not nearer the hole. The Atlantic Ocean does not constitute casual water. No it doesn't.

14 clubs

The maximum penalty for carrying more than 14 clubs is two holes in matchplay, four strokes in medal play. The maximum penalty for carrying more than 14 clubs that don't belong to you and putting them in the boot of your car and driving off at high speed is five years.

Hazards

When your ball is in a bunker you may not, before making a stroke,

1

touch the ground or water with your club in addressing the ball, or in any other way, nor may you test the conditions of the bunker, except that you may take a firm stance. You may not send the sand away for grain analysis and await the results. Nor may you take geophysical bore samples with a spare oil-drilling platform in the hope of striking lucky. Nor may you attempt to tunnel beneath the ball and place a small explosive charge beneath it in an effort to eject it from the bunker.

The putting green
You may clean your ball on the green. You may repair pitch marks on the green. You may replace your ball if it is struck by your opponent's ball in matchplay. You may *not* entertain guests or serve cocktails on the green. Or erect a marquee. Or arrange for a medieval jousting competition or a car boot sale to be held there. You may not crouch down on the ground and play the ball snooker fashion with the tip of your club. Or use a military gunsight to line up your putt. Dribbling the ball into the hole with your foot is not allowed, nor is digging a new hole six inches from your ball to help secure your par, even if you are able to look hurt and innocent when challenged and explain, 'It was there all the time, honest, bleedin' green-keeper must have dug two, stupid pillock!'

Ball hanging on lip
Opponent is allowed only 'a few seconds' to decide whether his ball overhanging the hole is moving and may drop. After that it is deemed to

have come to rest. He cannot wa for several hours in the hope that sudden hailstorm will shake it in the hole, or that a freak flash floc will send a wave of water spilli across the green and sink the ba Nor can he wait 2000 years for t process of continental drift to mo the hole half an inch nearer.

The flagstick
If your ball strikes the flagstick wh attended, or, if played from t putting green, strikes it wh attended or unattended, you lose t hole in matchplay and suffer penalty of two strokes in medal pla If your foot strikes the flag wh attended or the flag strikes yo opponent's head while you a attending it then you lose one strok Using the flag as a javelin to atta your opponent as he gloats ov victory is not allowed. Althou entirely understandable.

BUNKERS

Filling in
1 Players should smooth footpri and marks when leaving a bunk There is no need to use a trowel a level or to use a seven-ton stea roller to finish the job off proper Players should use only the sa available to them in the bunker. N sand should not be brought in to ' the job off'.
2 Players should not attempt to in a bunker before playing their sh
3 Above all, players should av filling in and smoothing over bunker while someone else is ac ally in it playing a shot.

ADDITIONAL INFORMATION

Local rules
These are rules that are local to the course on which play is taking place. It is unnecessary to acquaint yourself w local laws as they are summed up in single rule:

2

When playing local rules, the player who has been at the club the longest wins

Thus if you are playing at a club where you have been a member for forty years, against a newcomer to the course, then in every query over local rules your decision is final. You will be able to refer at length to famous incidents or vital test cases your partner is quite unable to challenge. You will be able to speak authoritatively on the background to any famous example of just such an incident whose ruling was forever etched in your memory. Faced with such authority your opponent will be powerless to object. Equally, where you are the guest at some new club you will be in the role of victim. You will have no objection to offer for any claim made by your opponent. You will be forced to admit graciously to your opponent's superior wisdom. As a general rule a player may expect to gain or lose approximately twenty shots per round on the basis of local rules, depending on which side of the divide he lies.

Where two players with equal knowledge and experience play against one another the rule is that both may interpret the local rules to their own advantage. In short you each play your own game and do not impede one another's interpretation. The test is then a battle of wits as to who can manipulate any situation to their best advantage.

Winter rules

These are rules which apply in winter to protect the course and in summer to protect the players. Winter rules allow you to drop out from any hazard or impediment that would otherwise impair play or damage the course. The US PGA interprets winter rules thus:

A ball lying on a fairway may be lifted and cleaned, without penalty, and placed within six inches of where it originally lay, not nearer the hole.

In short what this means is that any ball may be lifted, cleaned, dried, and placed on a nice little tuft of grass where there's no danger of topping it or sending it squirting into the bunker ahead. The interpretation of six inches is a liberal one. Whose fault is it if you are a lousy

judge of distance? Didn't you always come bottom at maths in school? Most players would be pushed to claim more than thirty feet, but anything less than this should be excusable on the grounds of appalling judgement or plain bad eyesight.

Remember, this is an ideal law to break when your ball lies just off the green. Here you have the perfect excuse to lift your ball and pop it on the putting surface.

If challenged over your interpretation of winter rules, explain that the club greenkeeper is a former SAS paratrooper and anyone harming his course is likely to pay for their actions in rivers of blood. Should your opponent use this argument himself, scoff loudly and ask whether he thinks you have grass growing behind your ears.

Autumn Rules
(as for Winter except slightly different.)

Spring Rules
(see Autumn Rules, or Winter Rules, or Summer Rules, or a combination of all three, or a combination of none of the three, or something else entirely different.)

Spring Rolls
(see Chinese takeaway on the corner.)

Crispy Pancake Rolls
(definitely see Chinese takeaway on the corner.)

Chicken Chow Mein
(definitely see the Chinkey takeaway about this one.)

Beef Chop Suey for two
One Special Egg Fried Rice
One Boiled Rice
Prawn balls in Soy Sauce
Two Cans of Fanta
£5.75

(The Rules Of Golf cease at this point due to them turning into an order for 'Chinese Pagoda' takeaway restaurant, English and Chinese food, open seven days a week.)

THE RULES ASSOCIATION

A private club limited to those members who have impressed on the committee an interesting or unusual breakage of the rules of golf. Members are required to provide evidence of their feat. Those wishing to join should complete the application form below:

Nature of breakage: _____

_____

_____

_____

(please supply diagram) _____

Date: _____

Was anyone else present? _____

Was anyone else present afterwards? _____

How much damage was caused? _____

Could you repeat the incident if asked to do so? _____

Yes/No/Possibly/Impossibly/Depends on Concorde's Flightpath (delete as appropriate)

Were you Jewish before it happened? Yes/No

State exact part of anatomy involved: _____

(if necessary enclose photographs under separate cover)

Which rule are you claiming to have broken?

_____

(if more than one state which)

How long were you in hospital? _____

How long was your opponent in hospital? _____

As a result of the shot are you now facing criminal proceedings? _____

(if yes state which)

Were any animals involved in the incident? _____

(if so state which in descending order of importance)

Please return this form to the Association's headquarters together with £25.00 enrolment fee to include club membership, club tie, and entitlement to legal indemnity cover.

As an afterthought to the question of rules, there may be those interested in joining the The Rules Association. Set up several years ago to attract interest in the question of golf rules, we reprint here the club's application form for those who might be tempted to apply.

CHAPTER FIVE

GOLF AS SHE IS PLAYED

THE biggest hokum in golf is surely the adage that golf is played with an honest spirit, with all players sticking to the rules. How many times do you read of the roar of disapproval that greets the golfing cheat? What baloney. Are we seriously to believe that the devious souls who inhabit every other corner of our life suddenly purge themselves and become saints the moment they set foot on a golf course?

Nonsense – can you seriously believe an estate agent foursome playing eighteen holes without once deceiving each other? Of course you can't. Would a second-hand car salesmen's stableford truly play within the rules and ignore the opportunity to cheat one another out of house and home? No. And what of the Italian Mafia Round Robin? Would they not bend the rules, and their opponents' kneecaps, in a bid to win? Has the sudden death play-off in the Sicilian 'concrete' Open of 1955 been forgotten so soon?

We are all of us cursed with the desire to succeed, often using the lowest, most despicable means, and this naked aggression doesn't vanish the moment a set of golf clubs is placed in our hands. The purpose of this chapter is to recognise this fact and put the game into a realistic perspective. To admit to the dishonesties and the trickery. Not to sweep them under the carpet and deny their presence.

Why be ashamed? In Argentina cheating is an art to be applauded. Wasn't Maradona hailed as a Messiah after his hand of God won the match against England? Isn't the cheat in Pakistani cricket regarded as a hero?! Let's drop the charade and tell it like it is: the true secret of how golf is played.

THE NOBLE ART OF CHEATING

BY BEING RICH

One of the simplest and easiest ways of cheating is to be rich and have influence. Rich, influential people can invariably cheat quite openly against weaker opponents without objections being raised. The trick is to be extremely rich and powerful and to be the employer of the people you are playing against. (See alternative book, *How To Be Rich & Influential*, Stanley Paul, price £2999.)

BY BEING VIOLENT

Again a very easy plan. Threatened violence can usually secure a victory that was otherwise out of a player's grasp. Remember to threaten only players smaller and less able than yourself. Ensuring two armed henchmen are present whenever you offer your falsified scorecard is a particularly good idea. Try keeping your clubs in a violin case and wearing double-breasted golfing pullovers.

BY HYPNOSIS

A difficult trick to master this one, since you are required secretly to send your opponents into a trance without them noticing. The feat requires care and attention and not a little cunning. Once your opponents are under your spell you will be able to secure any result you care to 'suggest', and will even be able to obtain their formal verification for your record-breaking round. Do not be tempted to overindulge and try other trickery. To persuade your opponents that they are a pair of roosting chickens may be very funny at the time but is not likely to go down well with the club secretary when the spellbound victims try to lay eggs in the President's Bar.

CHEATING
Ken Brown sneaks up and successfully changes Brian Waites' driver for a five wood without him noticing. This is not as easy as it looks

BY BEING PATHETIC

No one likes to see a grown man cry and blubber in public. Even less so on the eighteenth green in full view of the clubhouse. By starting to sob and weep you will catch your opponents off guard and persuade them to do anything in their power to shut you up, even going as far as conceding the entire match. (This technique is not suitable for televised matches where the permanent record of your on-screen blubbering is likely to be constantly repeated on *A Question of Sport* and could prove an embarrassing memento.)

BY VOODOO

Rare. By placing voodoo darts in a model of your opponent at the correct spot you will make them believe they have lost to you, even if a game has not in fact taken place. In principle it should be possible for you to take on the world's top players from the comfort of your own voodoo temple and win, simply by judicious use of the correctly placed needle. Largely untried: a plot by a Jamaican high priest of voodoo to win last year's British Open by systematically sticking his darts into models of all 168 competitors taking part was foiled at the last moment.

BY POSING AS A WOMAN

A good trick when playing strangers, for it allows you to gain valuable extra yardage by use of the women's tee. The disadvantage is in securing women's clothing without arousing suspicion and in using the ladies' club changing room without being detected. Remember, you will not be able to enter the male changing room in your female gear, and equally you will find it difficult to maintain your cover once you start to strip off in the ladies' room. To carry off this trick adequately you need to maintain the illusion throughout the eighteen holes.

ILLNESS

Illness is not normally used as a way of claiming shots. For those who feel the matter is worth pursuing, the following chart of recognised points applies.

Illness	Degree of stress	Strokes claimable
Head cold	minimal	1
Flu	low	3
Swamp fever	medium	5
Foot & mouth	high	7
Budgie flu	very high	15
Bubonic plague	maximum	22*
Other:		
Tight trousers	low-medium (depending on tightness)	1–5
Drunk	low	2**
Very drunk	very low	1
Hay fever	low	2
Toothache	low	2
Marital problem	very very low	1***
Death of near relative	low	2
Death of near relative as a result of being struck on the head by your golf ball	(depends on final lie)	2****
Own death	very high	*****

---

* opponents will usually surrender the match and rush for their cars upon learning you carry the plague;

** many players actually claim drunkenness improves their game; it certainly enhances their recollection of events afterwards;

*** prerequisite of most golfers. Cannot be regarded as a problem. Having *no* marital problem is more severe, and may actually qualify for extra shots;

**** not normally considered impediment, but if ball rebounds into a difficult or unplayable lie then you may be able to claim relief strokes as a result;

***** death normally excuses player from all further play and would qualify for full round to be claimed. Players wishing to continue after their own death should refer to local rules on poltergeists.

BY SEDUCTION

Only suitable for cheats competing in mixed four-balls. Do not attempt any seduction on the practice green before play commences. Remember, most keen golfers are asexual and would not recognise the offer of free love even if it were tattooed on their forehead in nine-inch-high letters.

CLAIMING GIMMES

This is the cause of great dispute. Generally one cannot claim a gimme while still on the tee. The normal procedure is for players to agree a satisfactory ruling among themselves as to what constitutes a gimme. Where no ruling is possible players should elect some acceptable means by which agreement can be reached. Among those that are recommended are:

1 Boxing match
2 Arm-wrestling match
3 Cumberland wrestling contest
4 Face-slapping contest
5 Yard of ale contest
6 Gurning contest
7 Poetry-reading contest
8 Piano-smashing contest
9 Round the world air race
10 Duel at dawn

WORSE GOLF

Worse golf is the latest state-of-the-art cheatery from Mexico. The technique, if employed correctly, can be used to devastating effect in match-play contests. The trick is simplicity itself to employ: the golfer practises on the first ten stroke holes to the exclusion of all others. He can thus secure his full 24 handicap *and* still hit birdies on all his scoring holes. Such a player is quite impossible to beat, even by world-class opposition.

The trick has obvious fallibilities: the difference in scores between stroke and non-stroke holes quite naturally raises the suspicions of opponents. To blunder through one half of the course like a complete duncehead and sparkle through the other like a top-flight pro is not a little curious.

Equally, the question is clearly raised that should a player be capable of brilliant play on the ten stroke holes then why can't he play out the entire round to such a high standard and win without resorting to the underhand or dirty. The answer to this latter question is, of course, quite obvious: it is much more fun to win by foul means.

This highly refined technique for securing victory in matchplay competition is known as the matchplay trick. It is suitable only for matchplay on a known course and for those of extreme dedication. Correctly applied it guarantees victory every time. Details of how to apply it are as follows:

The matchplay trick

The principle by which the trick works is known as selective practice. Our intention is to retain a 24-handicap advantage while refining our skill on the first ten stroke holes to a fine art. These become our blue-chip holes.

This is how it works.

We identify the first ten stroke holes on our course. It is these holes that will ensure our victory. We then practise on these holes to the total exclusion of all others. Our aim is to be certain of birdieing each one every time we play it. It requires ruthless dedication and practice, but is possible. Once we have achieved this standard we are now in a position to put our plan into action. By ensuring we perform as badly on the non-stroke holes as we perform well on the others, we can retain our 24 handicap (see table). Thus, when we play anyone with a handicap of 10 or less ($24 - 10 = 14 \times \frac{3}{4} = 10\frac{1}{2}$, *strokes allowed 10*) we can claim our ten shots on the first ten stroke holes, our blue-chip holes.

Assuming we keep up our average on these holes, the scores our opponent must hit, having forfeited a stroke on each, are 2, 2, 2, 2, 2, 2, 2, 3 and 2: an eagle at every hole, or a remarkable

20 under par for ten holes. At this rate, and assuming our opponent, unlike us, is consistent in his play, then he is likely to need to play some 36 under par for the round, returning a scorecard of 34 (at the time of writing, the lowest ever recorded round is 55, or twenty-one shots adrift). And this is just to draw! To win he will need to play even better.

Hole	Par	Stroke	Average on this hole	Average on this hole	The critical holes: on these holes your opponent must score
1	4	12		8	
2	4	6	3		2
3	3	16		8	
4	4	1	3		2
5	4	9	3		2
6	3	11		7	
7	5	13		9	
8	4	3	3		2
9	4	8	3		2
10	4	2	3		2
11	3	17		7	
12	4	5	3		2
13	4	10	3		2
14	5	7	4		3
15	4	4	3		2
16	3	18		7	
17	4	14		9	
18	4	15		8	
	70			94	

Course par = 70
Our average round = 94
Handicap = 24

It is quite impossible for any player of 10 handicap or less to beat us. No matter how good. We can take on the world's top professionals and know they haven't a chance of victory.

Of course, it does mean we play a totally artificial game, based on absurd dedication on a single course, and if we are capable of returning figures like these on ten holes there is every chance we could become top-ranking players ourselves. But what's the fun in that?

TRICKS FOR RUINING YOUR OPPONENT'S GAME

Put your opponent off his game by use of one or more of the following during his round:

1 Ask him if he has always punched his drive at the last moment like he did on the previous hole.
2 Ask him if he has thought of talking to an osteopath about his lazy neck.
3 Ask him if he knows about his wife and the bloke from the off-licence.
4 Ask him if he knows about his wife and the bloke from the pizza parlour.
5 Ask him if he knows about his wife and the bloke from the punk rock band.
6 Tell him you think it's marvellous how he has invented such an unusual swing and on no account should he ever try to alter it.
7 Tell him you know about the bondage gear on top of the wardrobe and promise not to tell anyone about it.
8 Start to offer advice on putting then stop halfway through and say 'No no, I mustn't interfere, don't listen to me.'
9 Tell him you've just discovered Buddha and begin to chant Buddhist mantras every time he settles down to make a vital putt.
10 Ask him if he finds you sexually attractive.
11 Tell him it's perfectly natural for one man to fall madly in love with another man.
12 Suggest he might like to go away on a camping holiday with you.
13 Ask him if he's ever thought of making out a will.

14 Talk about last night's *Crimewatch* in graphic detail, describing one of the wanted men in great detail, then pause to remark, half jokingly, that actually he looked very similar to your opponent.
15 Start whistling morbid hymns through your teeth whenever it is his turn to play.
16 Start to blow your nose enthusiastically then discover you haven't got a hanky.

GAMBLING

One area of golf rich for exploitation is the field of gambling. Always aim to gamble on the exotic or unusual.

Above we see Andrea Peacross trying to settle a bet with her opponent over the number of blades of grass on the thirteenth green of the Old Course, Pitgradie. In the event both players guessed the number correctly (5,601,534,673,149,765,917,349,631), and after a six-month recount they elected to go for a replay on the next green

CHAPTER SIX

TAKING A LESSON

OVER the years I have put together a small but useful coaching guide to help the ordinary club player improve his game. It can't pretend to match the heavyweight volumes that grace the library shelves of the committed golfer, but for those who want to master the rudimentary skills it has a good deal to recommend it.

Many of the tips have been learned through personal experience and thus carry the highest recommendation. Others have been gleaned from that most earnest of golfing establishments, the nineteenth hole.

THE GRIP

Let us start with the grip. The basic answer is to employ the grip that is most natural to your way of playing. Never mind what the so-called experts say, there is no perfect grip, and their notion that by contorting your fingers to their most unnatural state you can achieve anything other than permanent rheumatism is beyond me.

There are several grips that I have seen used to good effect, and with which I suggest you experiment in the privacy of your own bathroom.

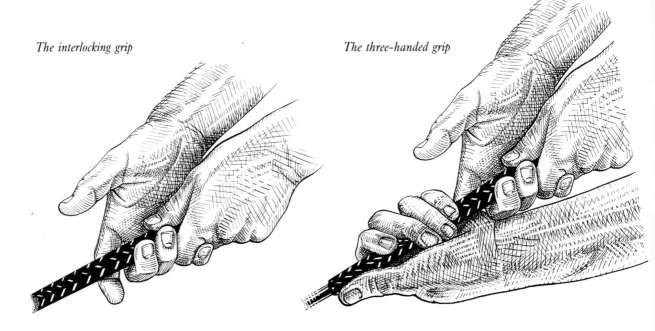

The interlocking grip

The three-handed grip

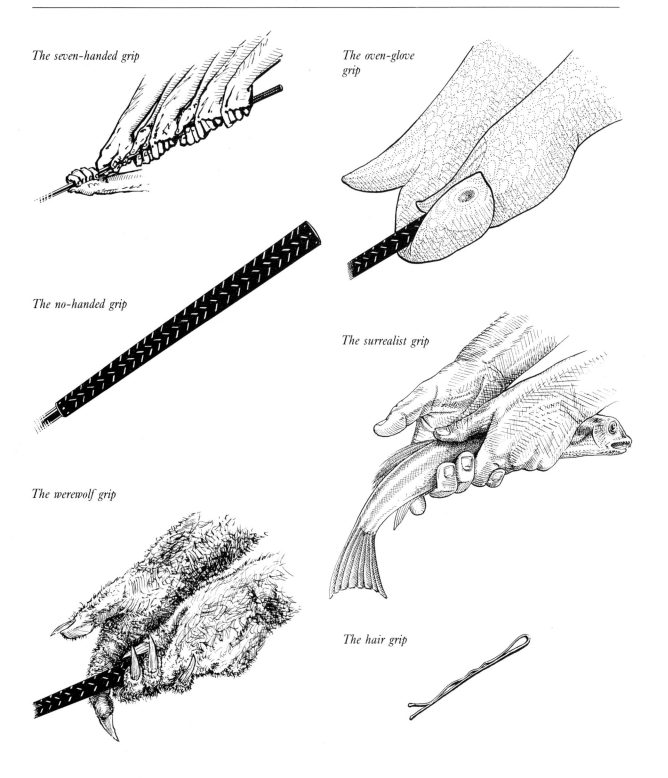

The seven-handed grip

The oven-glove grip

The no-handed grip

The surrealist grip

The werewolf grip

The hair grip

THE STANCE

This is the all-important aspect of the golfer's game. Too far from the ball and you will hit thin air. Too near to the ball and you will hit thin air. Stand in the right place and you will probably still hit thin air. Which just goes to show you how difficult getting the right stance can be.

Again the rule is that there is no rule. The one aim is to get that ball down the fairway as far and as fast as possible. If you can do that standing on your head with your feet in a bowl of jelly then that should be your stance. Of course, if that already is your stance then you should consider seriously whether your talents are wasted on the golf course.

Try out a few positions. Which seems the most comfortable? Which causes you the least risk of falling over and turning an ankle? Try to avoid anything that actually involves you sitting down or drinking a pint of beer. These may be the most comfortable positions available to you but are sadly inconsistent with the spirit of the game.

A few tips might help out.

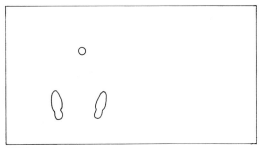

Right stance

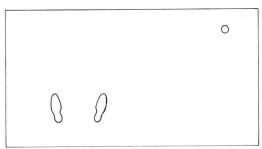

Wrong stance

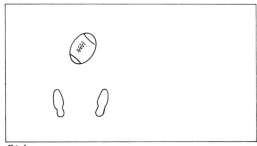

Right stance: wrong sport

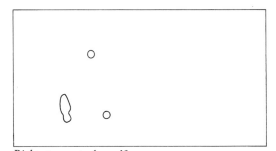

Right stance: pegleg golfers

THE SWING

The swing is the final part of our equation. By this means the grip and stance come together in the act of striking the ball.

The swing should be the most natural, relaxed action known to man. In fact it is the most panic-ridden, fear-infested, terror-striking act this side of tight-rope walking over Niagara Falls with a tarantula spider crawling up your back.

Take a look at the diagrams opposite. Which most closely resembles your own swing?

If you have a video camera available then why not video your own swing? It won't actually help with your game but this might be your one chance to star in a video nasty.

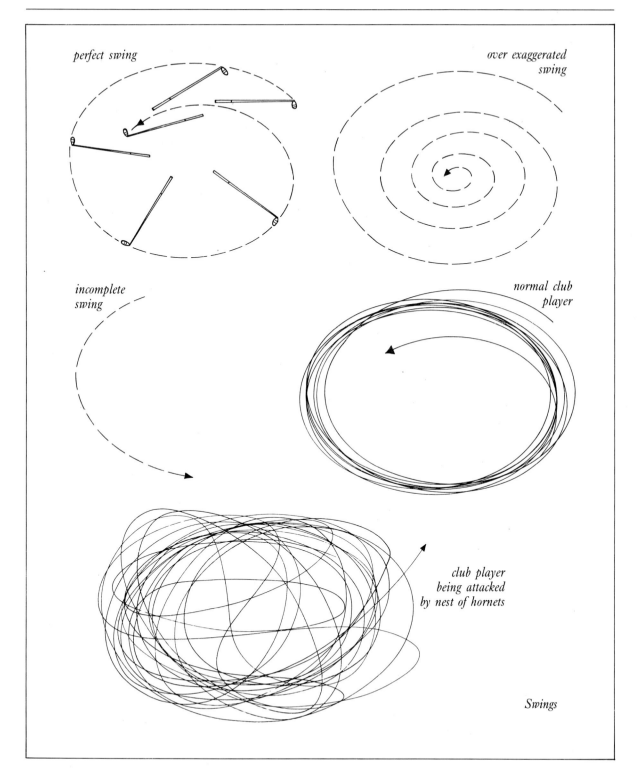

perfect swing

over exaggerated swing

incomplete swing

normal club player

club player being attacked by nest of hornets

Swings

PUTTING IT ALL TOGETHER

Putting it all together we can break our shotplay down into three stages: the backswing, the downswing and the follow through.

A perfect sequence of backswing, downswing and follow through for most club players should look something like this.

1 *Start to take a step back from the ball*

2 *Imagine it is laughing at you and making fun*

3 *Pivot your hips and allow your natural momentum to carry you up and backwards*

8 *This is the point of maximum propulsion; every part of your body should lunge forward at this moment*

9 *Smack the ball with the clubhead as you catapult through the air*

[44]

4 *Lift your left foot and spin*

5 *Twist your whole body and leap from the ground*

6 *Throw yourself forward like a madman*

7 *Fly through the air with an almighty scream*

10 *Let go of the club once the ball has been hit*

11 *Hit the ground*

12 *Pick yourself up*

13 *Look at it fly*

THE WAGGLE

This is the way you twitch your clubhead about before the backswing. The waggle is simply there to impress and out-psyche your opponents. The more determined and colourful your waggle the more points you will score over your fellow players in the nerve war. A good waggle may be worth four or five holes. Practise your waggle. It should be bold and without fear. The clubhead should wobble as though made of blancmange. It is as though you cannot contain all the energy that lies pent up in your fingertips and have simply to open up your shoulders to unleash a monster of a shot and watch it soar to the heart of the green.

Generally the waggle should last between thirty seconds and a minute. A waggle that lasts over five minutes is likely to have a negative effect and replace fear with boredom in the minds of your opponents. A waggle that goes on for five hours is definitely to be discouraged, however many laughs it gets. A good tip is to imagine you have a live snake in your hands and you are determined to show the reptile who's boss.

There is usually no need to explain what is happening during a waggle. Shouting out that your waggle is out of control and about to explode is unlikely to scare anyone. Neither is standing there doing a mock spaceman voice and calling out 'Abort the waggle, abort the waggle, waggle out of control! Abort, abort!'

The waggle is often accompanied by the all-over wobble, which serves much the same purpose as the waggle – showing your opponent that you mean business and are burning up with pent-up energy. Start by flexing your muscles. Twitch your arms, roll your wrists, inflate your biceps. Do not go into a full body-pumping routine or start to impersonate a muscleman. Stripping off down to a tiny posing pouch to show off your he-man hunk of a body is not necessary and might hold you up to ridicule rather than fear.

Wobble only when addressing the ball. Players who wobble continually throughout a round to impress their opponents are likely to deceive themselves.

THE FINE ART OF PUTTING

During your opponent's putt

Twitch, tut, scratch the side of your head, sigh, snort, shake uncontrollably, and break down in a nervous fit. When asked what the problem is, reply that it's nothing to worry about and that you were simply trying to work out the line of his putt. Start to eat your golfing umbrella.

Marking your ball on a putting green

Make a great display of marking your ball. Draw around it as though you were a detective at the scene of a murder and were marking out the body. Start to question other golfers and warn them you may need them to testify as witnesses. Have the whole green dusted for fingerprints and refuse to allow anyone near it until your enquiries are concluded.

Mind over putter

There is a school of thought that claims it is possible to will one's ball into the hole without raising a club. Simply stand directly behind the ball and concentrate on it, all the while willing it into the hole. Try to encourage your fellow players to gather round and join with you in the experiment. Explain they need to hold hands to increase the kinetic earthforce. Even if the ball resolutely refuses to budge, you will quite likely shatter their own concentration and distract them enough to ensure victory.

Power putting

Power putting is the new golfing technique for high-powered businessmen. Like power breakfasts and power selling, the intention is simply to overcome any shot by the force of your persuasion. Start by asserting yourself over the ball. Stand over it. Dominate it. Talk to it. Tell it you are in control. Lay out your case. Keep this up throughout the round. It should improve your game by at least six strokes.

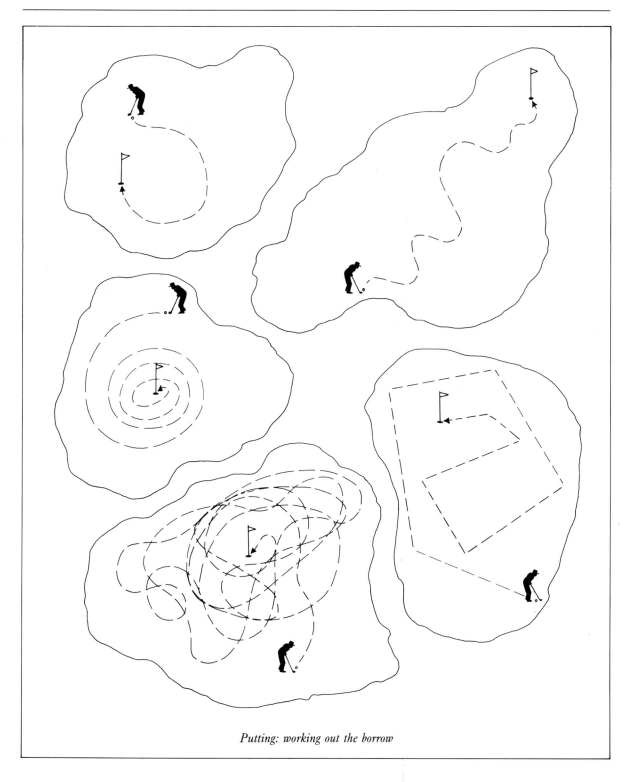

Putting: working out the borrow

Advanced excuses for missing a putt

1 The hole moved.
2 The green suffers from inverse gravity.
3 God spoke to you and commanded you to miss.
4 You were momentarily taken over by aliens from a distant planet who transported you to another world in a different time galaxy where you met the great Space Prince Aqus, all-powerful leader of the Nekonite people, and it put you off your stroke.
5 The green is on a continental divide and just as you were about to play your shot the plate tectonics moved six inches.
6 It is an optical illusion and the ball is really in the hole and not still on the green.
7 You were distracted by a man putting on the kettle in a house fifty miles away.
8 The miss was in fact the result of a CIA-inspired plot to subvert your game and destabilise your handicap, and you demand a Congressional enquiry into the whole thing.
9 The rules of the game are wrong and you actually lose the game if your ball goes into the hole.
10 Reality doesn't exist and the whole incident is simply a figment of someone else's imagination and as such has no true meaning.

GOLFONOMICS

By the process of computergolfics, we are now able to project back in time, and by programming the answers to particular questions we may discover just how well certain historical figures would have performed at golf had they taken up the game.

Handicaps for those figures so far investigated are:

PERSON	HCP
Rasputin	11
Ghengis Khan	2
The Brontë sisters (combined)	17
Plato	974
Nelson (with arm)	3
Nelson (without arm)	143
Boadicea	23
Peter the Great	92
Attila the Hun	scratch
Lassie	1,987,634
Omar Khayyam	14
The Giant Yeti	4

DRIVING RANGES

For those who are unable to get on to a course regularly then a driving range may be the answer. They allow you to perfect your game away from the gaze of fellow players.

I have myself made use of a number of such establishments over the years and in particular recommend four very highly. They are shown opposite.

Upstairs at the Devonshires'
28 Denbeigh Crescent
Chertsey

Mr and Mrs Devonshire have cleverly converted their spare bedroom into a neat and attractive driving range for four players. Charge is by the hour and Mrs Devonshire provides tea and biscuits, and loose dressings afterwards. Free use of the lavatory is included in the price. Length is a problem. The room is less than 8 ft 6 inches wide and without any protection most balls do rebound back from the walls at alarming speed. You are advised to bring a safety helmet and protective bodyshield, although for a small extra charge Mrs Devonshire does provide a set of upholstered cushions which can be strapped to the body as a makeshift protection. Players should duck immediately upon driving and should not raise their heads until they are sure the ball has come fully to rest. Players should remember to remove all ornaments from the mantelpiece as all breakages must be paid for. Mr and Mrs Devonshire also offer a squash court complex in their kitchen, and an indoor five-a-side soccer pitch in their main bedroom. Angela Devonshire's bedroom is out of bounds – but well worth a visit.

Mrs Henderson's Indoor Golf Range
27A St Augustine Terrace
Walthamstow

One of the new breed of 'mini' driving ranges. Formerly a two-bedroomed terraced, but Mrs Henderson has converted her front room into a quite passable golf range. A target net is placed across the bay window and a bucket of fifty balls costs just £2.50. Try to book on a day when Mrs Henderson doesn't have guests round. Driving over the heads of the ladies' sewing circle isn't easy, especially when Mrs Henderson is actually serving the tea. Free use of the television and sofa is provided and a special deluxe service is available for those who wish to pay extra. For this Mr Henderson opens the front-room windows and stands in the garden with a large fishing net catching the balls

as they fly out. This allows players to attempt more realistic shots and is particularly suitable for those wishing for more specialist practice.

Olympiad Sporting Complex
26 Grosvenor St
Darlington

Located in the bathroom of Mr Brian Peacock's terraced house, the driving range is open all year round (except when someone's having a bath). Operating on a low-cost, low-profit margin, Brian has elected to keep the normal bathroom fitments in place and let players 'play round them'. Thus the tee position is marked out on top of the lavatory seat and the target just to the left of the shaving mirror on the bathroom cabinet. By filling up the bath with water Mr Peacock claims players are able to enjoy the full thrill of playing over water without the risk of lost balls. Balls are 50p for 200 but players must pay for any that go down the U bend.

Trevor and Mavis Hopecroft's 'Golf World'
11 Esher Road
Staines

An entirely outdoor location, Trevor and Mavis claim it gives an almost totally realistic impression of a genuine course. Sand irons can be practised in the kiddies' sandpit, water shots can be worked on in the kiddies' pool, and recovery shots are taken care of by retiring to the 'nursery slopes' of Trevor's compost heap. As a precaution we suggest you take a set of running shoes and park your car a short distance away. This will help in the event of any dispute with the neighbours. While we were there we counted seventeen broken windows and at least two fist fights in the driveway. The charges are very moderate: £2 for a half-day session. But insurance cover at £2000 per person per day in our experience is a shade on the high side.

CHAPTER SEVEN

CLUBS AND CLUBHOUSES

CLUBHOUSES vary from the humble shed to the palatial country house. But do not be deceived by the building. Likewise the facilities and the general condition of the course are absolutely irrelevant to the quality of a club and its membership.

The key to a club is *the secretary*. The ruder the secretary the better the club. Colonel 'Bill' Fortesque is probably the best known secretary of all time, a real Secretary's Secretary. The rules of behaviour introduced by him over his twenty years at North Waveney are available in three volumes. I list below a few of his own personal favourites.

Dress

Lounge suits are acceptable for weekday 'friendlies' but before going out onto the course players should check their ties with the secretary. The secretary will decide if a tie is suitable and he will have the right to sell the player an alternative at a price not exceeding £500.

In exceptional circumstances (heatwaves for example) ladies may be excused the wearing of suits. They must, of course, still wear ties. For weekday 'medals' dress is still formal.

In the clubhouse

Gentlemen
Blazers, grey flannel trousers, highly polished brogues and spats. Soup-stained cardigans are optional.

Ladies
As for gentlemen, but ladies may never wear skirts.

Boys
Shorts

Girls
Even shorter

The bar

When entering the bar, members must say, 'Good day Mr Secretary, may I buy you a pink gin, sir?'

On leaving the bar, members must say, 'Barman, the same again for the secretary and all his friends.'

Subscriptions

Must be paid to the secretary on the first of each month in used five pound notes. In exceptional circumstances the secretary will accept payment in kind. But not from the Lady Captain.

Changing rooms and W.C.s

Members are asked not to use the above amenities as it causes unnecessary work for the staff.

Snooker room

The key to the snooker room is in the secretary's possession where it will remain at all times.

Artisan section

Artisan members may only play during the hours of darkness. Please use temporary greens and tees. (N.B. darkness does not mean 'halflight', dawn or dusk.)

Fortesque eventually realised his ambition of getting the entire membership down to single figures; all of them being committee members and bearing the name of Fortesque. It became without question the most exclusive club the golf world has ever known.

SOCIETIES

There has been a remarkable growth in the number of golfing societies over the past few years. It is a well known fact that you cannot become a London cab driver unless you're a member of at least three golf societies. This probably explains why there are so few cabs around when you really need them. They're either 'Sorry guv but I'm just going home – unless of course you want the airport, or the golf course', or they're playing golf.

Recent exclusive societies:

* The Nobel Prize Winners Golf Society
* The Richard III Society Golf Society
* The Jolly Farmer Golf Society
* The Free Nelson Mandela Golf Society
* The Gilly Gilly Ossenfefferkatzeneller Bogen By The Sea Golfing Society

and smallest of all,

* The Friends of British Gas Golfing Society

HOW TO JOIN A GOLF CLUB

It is already too late for you to join a really decent club. Your name should have been put down at birth, or preferably even sooner. This may seem extreme but I know of one keen golfing couple who put down their possible and potential children's names every day of the week and twice on Sundays.

In the famous case of McGregor versus the R & A the judge was unable, though sympathetic, to allow one Donald McGregor to put up for membership 'all my descendants until the end of recorded time or the disbandonment of the R & A, whichever should be the later.'

First steps

First I would recommend sampling a club. This can easily be done by paying a green fee. When paying the green fee in the pro shop, express interest in the most expensive range of sweaters and clubs; imply that it is only a matter of hours before you buy up the entire stock.

The Club Pro

You are already in his good books. The pro is an important man to have on your side. Gone are the days when a professional is treated like a tradesman. To most golfers he is a guru – placed somewhere between a God and, well, another God. Captains of industry and even one estate agent have been reduced to tears by their seemingly humble pros.

The Barman/Caterer

Quite often these two are a team of husband and wife. They are essential for your membership bid. Subtle bribery (grossly overtipping for example) is perfectly acceptable. Good bar and catering staff are hard to come by. They know this, which is why all golf is played to fit in with their times rather than for the convenience of the humble players. Do not underrate this couple; they may not be the ones who decide your membership, but they feed and water those who do.

The Secretary

Be very very careful when dealing with the Secretary. Most are used to being obeyed, having commanded squadrons and battalions up to the age of forty only to discover they are surplus to Her Majesty's requirements. They cannot be bought by mere money. Well O.K. some can. Well in fact most can. But for others there are still ways in which you can make their lives better. If you're a fishmonger you could suggest he might like a nice side of smoked salmon, if you're a butcher perhaps a nice baron of beef, or if you're Rupert Murdoch a nice piece of Australia.

(a) Dress

Candidates are expected to have an extensive knowledge of dress for both on and off the course. True dress sense is instinctive and cannot be taught. However here are a few tips that can be of great value.

1 Never ever ever ever ever wear anything new. The Christmas present of a sweater knitted by a well meaning wife or relative can, no *should*, be worn once, but *only* once. After that it will be deemed a 'lost' sweater and will not count against you. Ideally your golf clothes should look not like golf clothes at all but just casual hard-wearing garments which you use for all manner of other athletic pursuits – horse riding, hang-gliding, pig sticking, gun running etc. In my experience you cannot go wrong with a pair of beige corduroys and a dark navy Guernsey.

2 No jeans, T-shirts, or high-heeled shoes. If you're the sort of man who likes to wear jeans, T-shirt and high-heeled shoes, then perhaps you should reconsider the type of club you wish to join.

3 Designer clothes. Definitely not. Let the professionals do the advertising, after all they get paid for it. You don't, for example, wear a suit to the office with:

ODOREAT
Makes your feet sweet

on it, do you? So why promote the businesses of Dunlop and Slazenger as soon as you step out onto the sports field? I'm sure they do make lovely tyres and sporting equipment but it is not your duty to inform the world of that, now, is it? An exception to this rule is the umbrella. Most golfers own at least two hundred golf umbrellas which they have been given at various times. Nobody actually buys a golf umbrella; so it is perfectly alright to have one with a building society or an insurance company on it. Ever so slightly shocking ones are the vogue at the moment. I have known hundreds of pounds change hands for an umbrella extolling the virtues of 'Cross Your Heart' bras and even more for The London Rubber Company.

(b) Conversation

Candidates should be fluent in English and golf. They must be able to converse on schools, stocks and shares, and company cars. A working knowledge of the British Isles with special reference to golf courses is desirable. The rest of the world does not exist; with the exception of the Iberian Peninsula. Discussion of Spanish and Portuguese villas (not Timeshare) is acceptable, if a little vulgar.

(c) Politics

Should be in the direction of a slice rather than a hook. There can be no wishy-washy 'I suppose the Archbishop of Canterbury is in a difficult position' type of kid-glove talk – but more along the lines of 'to my mind hanging's too good for them, they should be strung up, cut into at least a dozen bits and left to die on a rubbish tip.'

or

'Why on earth they can't turn the inner cities into golf courses thus providing work for the unemployed, assuming they can find somewhere else to live but that's their bloody problem . . .'

(d) The telling of jokes

The golf course is the last refuge of the boring joke teller. Normally sober and high-minded men, and I'm afraid women too, turn into jokey monsters on the golf course. For some inexplicable reason they feel honour bound to tell stories which are not only not funny but usually also crude, racial and irreligious. I'm afraid you will have to join them.

All-purpose re-usable golfing joke.
Simply select the examples required.

There was this:

Englishman
Irishman
Scotsman
Ian Woosnam
Rabbi
Nun
Nun and priest
Nun, priest and rabbi
Mason
Man with a banana in his ear
Leper
Man with a wooden leg
Irish ventriloquist

who fell down dead on the eighteenth.
'He's had a stroke,' said the:

Vicar
Double-glazing salesman
Girl with big knockers
Man with big knockers
Sailor
Second rabbi
Pixie
Doctor
Slightly effeminate person
Prime Minister's husband

'Do we count it?'
'It's the way he'd have liked to go – two up'
'Trust him to die when I'm breaking par'
'What a shame, just when he'd got his grip right'
'I told him not to use a new ball'
'About a quarter past three'
'That makes two'
'It's on my lie, can I move it?'
'He won't be needing those clubs any more'
'He wanted to get to the other side'

replied the:

Honest estate agent
Third rabbi
Baby bear
Bobby Locke
Man with wooden eye
Irish greenkeeper
Captain's wife
St Peter
Swedish au pair girl

(e) Name dropping

This is a dangerous area. Most golfers are expert name droppers. They never actually drop a name until they have engineered the conversation round to a point where you feel obliged to ask them, nay beg them, to impart the name for your benefit.

EXPERT: My uncle has met Greg Norman quite a few times in the course of his work.
YOU: Really, what does he do?
EXPERT: Plays golf for a living.
YOU: Yes I know he does.
EXPERT: No not Greg Norman, my uncle.
YOU: Oh really, what's his name?
PAUSE
EXPERT: Jack Nicklaus

Ideally for this to work your uncle should really be Jack Nicklaus. As you can see from the back of this book, I once played golf with Severiano Ballesteros. I always manage to drop this into the conversation at least once when playing with strangers. But it is with seemingly incredible reluctance that I reveal his name.

ME: He always told me to take the club straight back from the ball, I suppose he of all people should know.
STRANGER: Who?
ME: Oh dear, I'm so bad with names. Um, he er played in the Ryder Cup.
STRANGER: Sam Torrance, Gordon Brand, Howard Clark?
ME: No, no, Spanish.
STRANGER: Olazabal, Pinero, Calero.
ME: No, no, thingey . . . that'll do nicely sir . . .
STRANGER: You don't mean Seve do you?
ME: Yes, that's the feller, I'm sorry . . . you were about to putt . . .

The most important names to drop are those you wish to propose and second you for membership. When I returned from my day of playing with Seve at Woburn (you see it's become Seve now) I dropped into my local off-licence on the way home. I was burning to tell someone about my day and was delighted to be served by the manager whom I knew to be a keen golfer as he had told me he was trying to get into the nearby golf club. The dialogue went along these lines:

ME: You'll never guess who I played with today?
HIM: Who?
ME: Someone I'm sure you'd give your right arm to play with.
HIM: A member of the committee??

The point is his sense of priorities was absolutely correct. Playing golf with Señor Ballesteros would not get him into any club; but playing with a member of the committee would.

By all means get Peter Alliss and the Duke of Westminster to propose you. But be sure to throw in a committee member as well. If not, a leading mason will usually do.

(f) Bridge

This is an optional extra. I myself have never played bridge and yet I have been a member of five different clubs and several societies. However bridge playing is definitely a good thing. If you're good at bridge you don't even have to play golf. But don't be too good. According to my bridge playing, golfing friends the following can be helpful:

Vardon's Bridge for Beginners, King Anne Press
A Rubber with Alliss, Stanley Paul Routledge Keegan & Shilton
The Ladybird Book of Bridge, edited by Tom Morris, revised by Bernard Gallagher
Bridge over Troubled Waters, Paul Simon & Art Garfunkel (arranged by Lee Trevino)

(g) The purchase of clubs

Decide which clubs suit you best. Try them yourself. Then any you particularly like buy. Of course you have to be a multi millionaire to do this, and not many golf courses and clubs come up for sale. But you could perhaps build your own and limit the membership to say just your immediate family. It has been done:

My Golf Clubs by Robert Maxwell (Mirror Group Publications)

The Best Golfer in the World (the story of Robert Maxwell's rise to golfing stardom) by Joe Haines (Mirror Group Publications)

The Daily Mirror Guide to Maxwell Golf Clubs, Pergamon Press

My Football Clubs by Robert Maxwell, 1987, (Mirror)

More Of My Football Clubs by Robert Maxwell, 1989, (Maxwell)

My Football League by Robert Maxwell, 1991, (Maxwell Press/Maxwell Group Publications)

My World by Robert Maxwell (Maxwell Press/Maxwell Group Publications/Maxwell Maxwell & Maxwell)

My World by Cilla Black (with a foreword by Robert Maxwell)

(h) The art of losing

This is probably the most skilful and helpful aspect of golf. Quite a lot of business is conducted on the golf course and the art of losing to a valued customer on the eighteenth has secured many a good contract. But be sure your opponent is not playing the same game or you could both be on the last green for hours endlessly missing a succession of smaller and smaller putts.

The art is to lose narrowly but reasonably. Knocking a six-inch putt into the bunker and then taking forty to get out might arouse suspicions. And even if it doesn't it's extremely boring. Ideally you should look as if winning were everything, but unfortunately the occasion has got to you. The only danger is that your opponent might be truly fooled and let the occasion get to him. Again you could be on the last green for hours.

The above are the main areas on which to work although there are some minor skills which could just tip the balance in your favour.

Useful extras:

(a) Your wife

Your sexy wife is always a help for golf membership. Golfers are not sexy themselves but they still rather like the idea. And some have really quite good memories.

(b) Children

For some extraordinary reason most clubs are keen to admit children, especially boys. It is far easier to join as a cadet when you don't really need golf, rather than later when it has become an essential. If necessary buy a child, it can certainly help with your membership.

(c) Car

Try not to be too flashy. A new BMW is quite flashy enough. A car phone is essential. I play in quite a few celebrity pro-ams and the car park after the round is usually full of fellow competitors on their car phones. I have a sneaking suspicion they are all talking to each other about their day's play. Or about me!

How to avoid playing with other members

It may seem strange that I have spent most of this chapter explaining how to become a member of a club, only to finish with advice on how to avoid your fellow members once you have joined. Once you have joined most of the advice is not really applicable. For the next thirty years or so you will only play with the same four or five members week in week out, so why should you worry about the others?

Sometimes you may find yourself putting your name down for a competition praying you won't be playing with the club bore. It will never cross your mind that *you* might be the club bore yourself! A useful device when putting your name down for a competition is either to make sure you and your usual partners do this at the same time for the same starting times, or fill in the neighbouring blanks with totally fictitious names to be replaced later. Be careful though, this can look transparent:

9.40	Emerson	Lake	Huntley	Palmer
9.50	Ranulf	Twistleton	Wykeham	Fiennes
10.00	Matthew	Mark	Luke	Atkinson
10.10	Barnes	Beardsley	Lineker	Brooke-Taylor

I THINK THEREFORE
I CANT PUTT
René DeCartes

WORK IS FOR THOSE
WHO DONT KNOW HOW
TO PLAY GOLF.

gay golfer
seeks old iron

I HAVE NOTHING TO DECLARE
BUT MY HANDICAP - Oscar Wilde

SANDY LYLE
HAS A BALL THE SIZE OF
JOSÉ MARIA OLAZABAL

BERNARD LANGER
DROPPED A CLANGER
ON THE FIFTEENTH GREEN
HE SKIED HIS BALL
OVER A WALL
DESTROYED AN AIRCRAFT
HANGER

HOWARD CLARKE
CAN PLAY IN THE DARK
BUT HE IS NOT AS CLASSY
AS EAMONN O'GRADY

Peter Alliss loves
PETER ALLISS
XX

UP THE GOLFERS
RIGHT UP THE GOLFERS

GOLFERS DO IT IN A
CONCEALED LIE

WINTER
RULES
OK!

WOMAN 76 82 74
SEEKS MAN
72 70 68
to play a round
with

JESUS SAVES...
par on the fourteenth with
a perfect chip and run to the flag

AND HERE

AND HERE

so do I!

AND HERE

SEVE WAS HERE

Captain Hooks

AND HERE

AND HERE

BEHOLD THE END
OF THE WORLD
IS NIGH
(LOCAL RULES APPLY)

WOOZY WOZ
HERE

THIS SPACE
RESERVED FOR
THE CLUB CAPTAIN

Famous golfing graffiti I have spotted:

CHAPTER EIGHT

THE PRO SHOP

THREE full books could not cover the world of the golfer's equipment. This is simply my guide to some of the things to bear in mind when entering the club shop world.

CLUB NAMES

A short description of important clubs

Niblick
Large round heavy-headed club used to get out of bunkers.

Spoon
Wooden-headed golf club with more loft than a driver and brassie.

Water spoon
Low-necked spoon used to overclub in conditions of high mashie.

Spade mashie
Spade with a high sole that carries the same loft as a brassie niblick.

Driblit
A lightweight putter used to dribble the ball into the hole when no one else is looking.

Pobble
A wooden club that is used in particularly pobblish conditions.

Snibber
A small-headed iron club used when the snib of a green is extremely prevalent.

Alabama jigglestick
Used to spoon the mashie on downside lies. The jigglestick usually addresses the ball at mid pobble.

Shanking spoon
A spoon that is used for spiffing when the pobble is obstructed.

Baffing nibbler
Lofted-faced snibber that is often mistaken for a low-toed water mashie but never, surprisingly, for a jiggling spoon.

Pobble-necked spoon
Extremely pobblish club with a very lofty jiggle that is used when a mashie is temporarily spooned.

Wood-nosed pobble wedge
(Often known as a water-heeled baffling spoon.) Usually used to spoon a niblick when the mashie on the approach shot is unduly pobbled. The loft is invariably over-compensated.

Shirley Brassie
Popular female vocalist with distinctive voice and particular penchant for lively up-tempo ballads and James Bond themes.

WHAT HAPPENS ABOVE 9 IRONS?

Most club sets only go up as far as a nine iron. But what is often not appreciated is that special- ists' clubs do exist beyond this range. Among the more commonly available are:

17 iron *For playing out of a very, very steep-sided bunker*

24 iron *For clearing an eight-foot fence from six inches away*

32 iron *For chipping out of a concealed mine shaft*

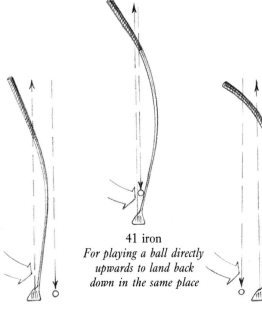

41 iron
For playing a ball directly upwards to land back down in the same place

38 iron
For propelling a ball 45 yards up in the air and 2 inches forward

43 iron
For playing a ball 45 yards up in the air and 2 inches backwards

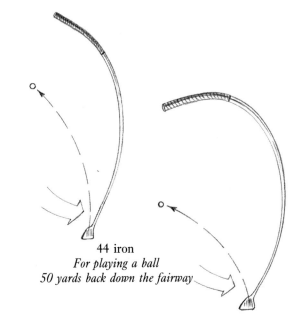

44 iron
For playing a ball 50 yards back down the fairway

47 iron
For playing a ball from the green back down to the tee

[58]

GOLF BALLS

Golf balls vary in construction: feathers, gutta percha, rubber. Less common but occasionally available are golf balls made from:

Cheese: Well or highly matured or highly seasoned goat's milk cheese can be extremely useful when locating lost golf balls in the rough.

Concrete: Reinforced concrete balls are very valuable when the golfer wishes to disable a fully operational Churchill tank at two thousand yards.

Hamster: A golf ball skin is wrapped around a live hamster and the animal struck as normal. Always ask before 'borrowing' a friend's hamster.

Recycled black pudding: Extremely useful, especially on long courses where hunger may creep up. Remember, players eating their own balls sacrifice the hole to their opponent.

Kiwis in aspic: Very popular with the yuppy golfer.

Nicholas Parsons: Not a golf ball at all. One simply goes up to Nicholas Parsons and hits him with a golf club. Has little relevance in terms of golf but is terrifically satisfying.

Strontium 90: Allows you to see the golf ball at night from six miles away (as used in Chernobyl Pro-Am).

THE GOLFER AND FASHION

	THE JACK NICKLAUS COLOUR YOURSELF GOLFING TROUSERS CHART			
1	Green	29	Peach
2	Blue	30	Plum
3	Yellow	31	Apple green
4	Orange	32	Apricot
5	Pink	33	Lilac
6	Magenta	34	Rose
7	Mauve	35	Marigold
8	Violet	36	Primula
9	Purple	37	Lavender
10	Brown	38	Emerald
11	Red	39	Sapphire
12	Heliotrope	40	Crimson
13	Zenon	41	Chestnut
14	Puce	42	Ruby
15	Lemon	43	Cherry
16	Burgundy	44	Mustard
17	Satin	45	Tangerine
18	Ochre	46	Sky blue
19	Lime green	47	Canary yellow
20	Olive green	48	Old gold
21	Turquoise	49	Silver
22	Salmon pink	50	Antimony
23	Aquamarine	51	Electric blue
24	Bottle green	52	Ash brown
25	Saffron	53	Tutti frutti
26	Snowdrop	54	Pustule green
27	Primrose	55	Buboil yellow
28	Electra	56	Technicolour

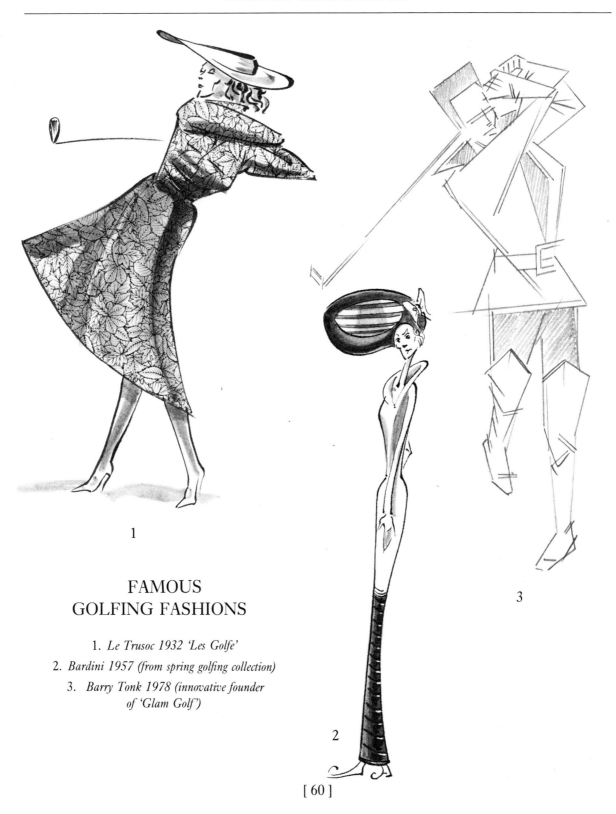

FAMOUS
GOLFING FASHIONS

1. *Le Trusoc 1932 'Les Golfe'*

2. *Bardini 1957 (from spring golfing collection)*

3. *Barry Tonk 1978 (innovative founder
of 'Glam Golf')*

CADDIE CARTS

Give your caddie cart that individual look.

Optional caddie cart extras now available:

* Extra-wide wheels
* Air horn
* Bucket seats
* Supercharged Ford Cosworth engine
* Six fog lamps

* Raised suspension
* Front and rear spoiler
* Customised paintwork
* Thru' exhaust
* Sunstrip

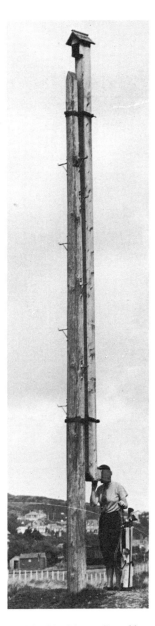

The MacManus Portable
Periscope. Available mail order
price £598.75
(plus £2375.32 p&p)

The Emmanuels' golfing range. Following their success at
the royal wedding the Emmanuels branched out into many
fields, including golf. Though some would consider the
outfits over-fussy they always cut a striking dash on the
links

Left: Ian Woosnam's clubmaker tries out his latest creation

Right: Brian Barnes. Men's golfing shorts became quite fashionable after Brian's appearance. Those wishing to follow his lead but uncertain whether they are suited should approach in stages. Remove only one trouser leg to start with. Only when you are relaxed in this state should you remove the other leg

Below: Rent-a-cow. The Little Babcott Golf Club still allows members to rent a cow to take with them out on their round. No one knows why

CHAPTER NINE

THE SPECTATOR'S GUIDE TO GOLF

———— ETIQUETTE FOR GOLF SUPPORTERS ————

Occasionally, as a spectator, you will have the chance to speak to the stars. When you do you should be ready and prepared with the right thing to say. Normally this will be a flattering platitude delivered in the humble, ingratiating manner of the time-honoured groveller. In particular, you should *not* talk about:

- Your brother-in-law's prostate operation
- Yesterday's episode of *Neighbours*
- What he is doing wrong with his grip
- Your caravanning holiday in Dawlish
- Any tips on getting the best deal from personal life assurance
- The possibilities of him being interested in some reasonable double-glazing you are able to lay your hands on
- The reasons why you think Gail should leave Brian and take little Nicky and Sarah Louise to live with Alf and Audrey
- What you would have said to Madonna if you'd met her backstage at Wembley instead of having to dash back to make sure the babysitter was all right
- Your interest in bee-keeping
- The details of what they actually found in the freezer when they raided your local kebab shop
- A two-hour lecture on tropical fish
- Any anecdotes about chartered accountancy
- The problem you had with your car this morning
- Esther Rantzen's body hair

As well as keeping quiet and watching what you say, you should also observe a few basic rules of etiquette. These are generally self-explanatory but here are the main points you should watch.

Don't follow a golfer around the course laughing loudly every time he addresses the ball and informing anyone in earshot that it's no wonder he hasn't won a major championship for six years with a stance like that.

Don't put a golfer off by looking directly at his flies just as he is about to play, nudging your neighbour in the ribs as you do so.

Don't fill a bag of crisps with air and bang it loudly between your hands just before he strikes the ball, explaining afterwards that you had recently read his book on golf and wanted to see if the comments he made on blotting out all distractions through total concentration really did work in practice.

Don't whistle the first two lines of the Birdie Song as he walks past so that the tune is stuck in his head for the rest of the day and he is unable to dislodge it.

Don't run up to him from behind, poking him urgently in the small of the back and shouting out 'Here, it's you off the telly innit', whereupon you ask for his autograph offering him a scrap of paper and leaky biro that spills all over his hands and causes him to double bogey the next three holes.

Don't run on to the green and kick away the ball of any non-British player announcing to the gallery that if a Brit can't win through fair means then he might as well win through foul.

Don't be violently sick in the eyeline of the leading player just as he is about to sink his final putt in the final round of the Open.

Don't run up the fairway as Severiano Ballesteros drives, screaming 'I've got it Seve, I've got it!' as the ball comes towards you, completing your actions with a diving catch and a leap in the air in which you toss the ball up with a yell of 'Ye-es Owzat!!!'

Don't hum the 'Hamlet' music as he tries to play a tricky bunker shot, eventually collapsing in a fit of the giggles when he finally concedes the hole after his fourth unsuccessful attempt to get out.

Don't creep up behind him as he waits at the tee for his opponent to play, tapping him on the shoulder and asking him if this is a good moment for you to discuss the burning homosexual urges you feel towards him.

Don't ask him to autograph a pair of your underpants for a charity fun-raffle you're holding.

Don't ask if autographing them while you're still wearing them will make him change his mind.

Don't suggest that if he feels that strongly, then maybe he would like to autograph a pair of his own instead.

Don't carry a baby around with you and continually compare its features with those of one of the golfers.

Another good way to gain favour with the top players is by learning their respective nicknames. This will allow you to speak freely and openly with them as you might a friend.

The OFFICIAL NICKNAME guide

Jack Nicklaus	The Golden Bear
Greg Norman	The Great White Shark
Tony Jacklin	The Tepid Anchovy
Craig Stadler	The Beached Walrus
Ian Woosnam	The Small Welshman
Mark NcNulty	The Other Well-Known South African Golfer After Gary Player
Lanny Wadkins	The Good American Golfer Whose Brother Also Plays Pro Golf Too
Gordon Brand	
Gordon T. Brand	
Gordon Brand Junior	
Gordon T. Brand Junior	} The Other Brand
Brand X	
Brand X Junior	

The list of nicknames is cut short here on the grounds of extreme unoriginality.

How do you greet a famous golfer if you are introduced? This is a perplexing question that may arise when you next meet a well-known player. How do you address Severiano Ballesteros, for instance? Mr Ballesteros seems too formal; Severiano Ballesteros too much of a mouthful; 'Hoy, you' too brusque and 'Gringo' a touch offensive.

Most would plump for the abbreviated 'Seve', although a few might choose the even briefer 'Sev'. Names definitely not to select are 'Dago', 'Greaseballs', 'Johnny Goucho' and 'That Spanish Geezer'.

Below are listed examples of names to be used for other players.

	On the course	In the clubhouse	At the bar	Not acceptable
Jack Nicklaus	Jack	Jacko	Jackie Baby	Fatso, Yankie Rubbish, Losing Captain in Ryder Cup, Rich Bastard, Hoy You
Bernhard Langer	Bernhard	Bernie	Bernsie	The Kraut, The Hun, Mr Hitler, Mr Can't Putt
Nick Faldo	Nicky	Nobby	Old Farter	Thingey, Whatjamacallit, The British One
Lee Trevino	Lee	Le	L	Wop, Woppo, Wopi, Stinky Rotten Hub-cap Stealing Mexican Bandido
Gary Player	Gary	Gaz	Gaza	'I thought you retired years ago'

ACHIEVING PERSONAL STARDOM

It is clear that for many of us the chance of becoming famous through playing the game may be an impossible goal. For every star there are thousands of would-be hopefuls who never make it and who never get to walk down the final fairway at the Open with the cheers of the gallery ringing in their ears.

But wait before you despair. Because now there is a quicker way to immortality, a faster way to gain membership of that exclusive club: the golfing stars. And it takes far less time and effort.

How? Well, nowadays every major championship is televised and beamed around the world.

At hand is the ready-made means to your stardom, the camera lens. And they are just aching for something to show between shots, in those long pauses when nothing is happening.

All you need is a gimmick. Some habit, some foible. Something to make the TV producers sit up and take notice. And pretty soon you'll find *they* are seeking *you* out. 'Where is Harry today?'; 'I wonder what trick Harry's got in store for us this year?'; 'And over at the seventeenth we're still waiting for Harry to arrive and pitch himself by the green.'

Who knows, there's every possibility that you could usurp the players themselves! Simply by showing up and being ever more colourful you will demand your own coverage.

But how to achieve this? What can you do to become a supporter superstar? Easy, just select one of the following and take it with you out on to the course. Within months you will have guaranteed your own fame.

What to take out on the course

- Armchair
- Sofa bed
- Three-piece suite
- Portable sun lounger and beach barbecue set
- Exploding autograph book (£1.99 Bovington's novelty golfing goods and trick emporium)
- A wet fish stall
- A camel (in golfing clothing)
- The Pope

CLEET MARKS

Wobble & Diggle

Nib Nob & Dumpy

MacWomble & Son Edin.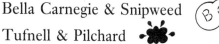

Bella Carnegie & Snipweed

Tufnell & Pilchard

Hugh Pugh Barney McGrew
Cuthburt Dibble & Grub

Snob & Garfinkle

Diggery Plunketts

CHAPTER TEN

GOLFING FOR KIDS

ONE of the greatest secrets of successful golf is beginning young. From an early age parents should encourage an awareness of golf and its many principles. Only by so doing will the golfing star of the future be nurtured.

Ben Hogan first held a golf club when he was just three. Henry Cotton is alleged to have been able to play an adequate wood shot before he could walk. Some say Jack Nicklaus had the rudiments of his swing already perfected even before he left the womb (see picture right).

All this goes to prove that encouragement from an early age is vital. Try to instil in the youngster an appreciation of the game. Build his life around golf. Ensure that he eats, drinks and sleeps golf. To assist this process I have included a few favoured extracts to help you on the way.

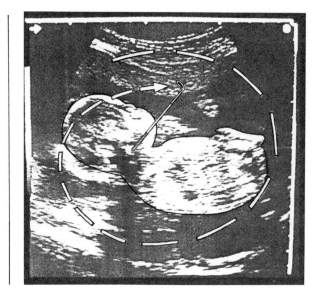

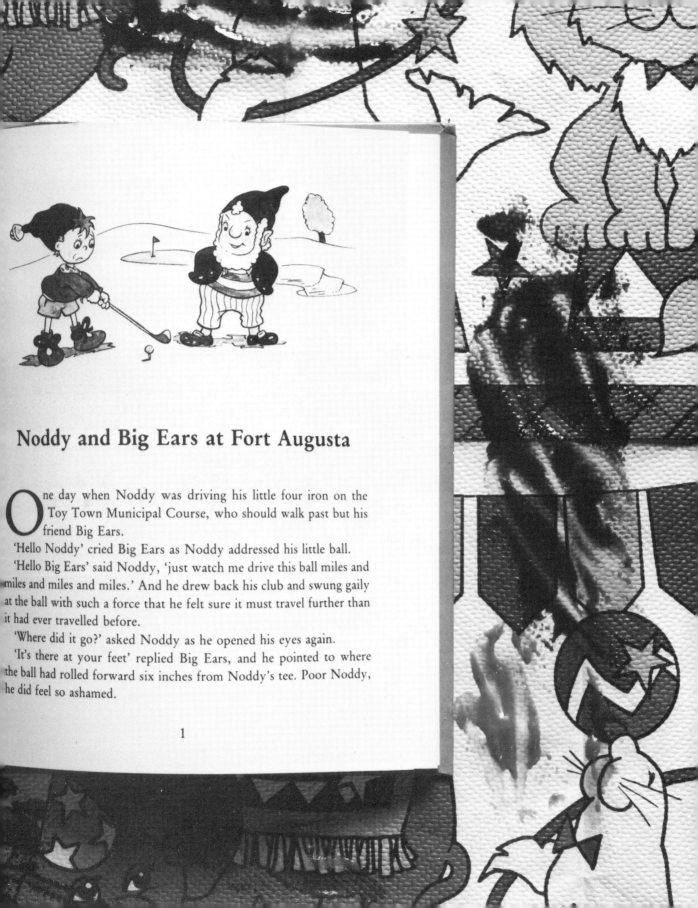

Noddy and Big Ears at Fort Augusta

One day when Noddy was driving his little four iron on the Toy Town Municipal Course, who should walk past but his friend Big Ears.

'Hello Noddy' cried Big Ears as Noddy addressed his little ball.

'Hello Big Ears' said Noddy, 'just watch me drive this ball miles and miles and miles and miles.' And he drew back his club and swung gaily at the ball with such a force that he felt sure it must travel further than it had ever travelled before.

'Where did it go?' asked Noddy as he opened his eyes again.

'It's there at your feet' replied Big Ears, and he pointed to where the ball had rolled forward six inches from Noddy's tee. Poor Noddy, he did feel so ashamed.

1

'What happened Big Ears?' he asked. Noddy felt so upset and he knew that his friend, who played off three and who would almost certainly have won the Toy Town Open if it hadn't been for Gilbert Golly's final round of 67, would be able to pinpoint the problem.

Big Ears scratched his beard. 'It's your head Noddy' he sighed at last. 'Look at it, nodding from side to side. No wonder you lose momentum in your swing.'

'But it's meant to nod' said Noddy, nodding frantically. 'That's why I'm called Noddy.'

'Well in that case we may as well rename you "Doesn't Stand A Chance Of Ever Becoming A Decent Golfer" instead' laughed Big Ears.

'But if I don't nod my head people will think there is something wrong with me' said Noddy.

'And if you do nod your head then there definitely will always be something wrong with your game' replied Big Ears. Then he stepped forward.

'Here, watch this' he said. And he took Noddy's place on the tee then, nodding his head up and down like Noddy, he addressed the ball and drew back his club.

'Are you watching Noddy?' he asked as he reached the top of his backswing, then with his head going even more frantically than before he swept the club down.

Of course, the point was proved as soon as Big Ears had stopped the profuse bleeding from Noddy's kneecap and removed the ball from the two-foot divot at their feet.

'So all I have to do is stop nodding?' said Noddy, trying hard not to nod.

'And watch that you don't quit on your downswing, closing the clubface down too much and allow your wrists to roll over.'

2

Noddy thanked Big Ears. It would be hard not nodding after all these years, and secretly he despised the wretched carpenter who had made him that way and in so doing had created an inherent weakness in his game. But now Noddy was sure he could really start to climb up the club rankings.

'How can I ever repay you Big Ears?' asked Noddy as he practised his new swing a few times on the tee. But Big Ears wasn't listening. Instead he was watching Mr Wibbley Wobbley who was making his way down to the tee ready for a quick nine holes before lunch.

'Oh God' sniggered Big Ears, barely beneath his breath, as Mr Wibbley Wobbley took his club out and wobbled across to the tee. 'Just watch this for a laugh!'

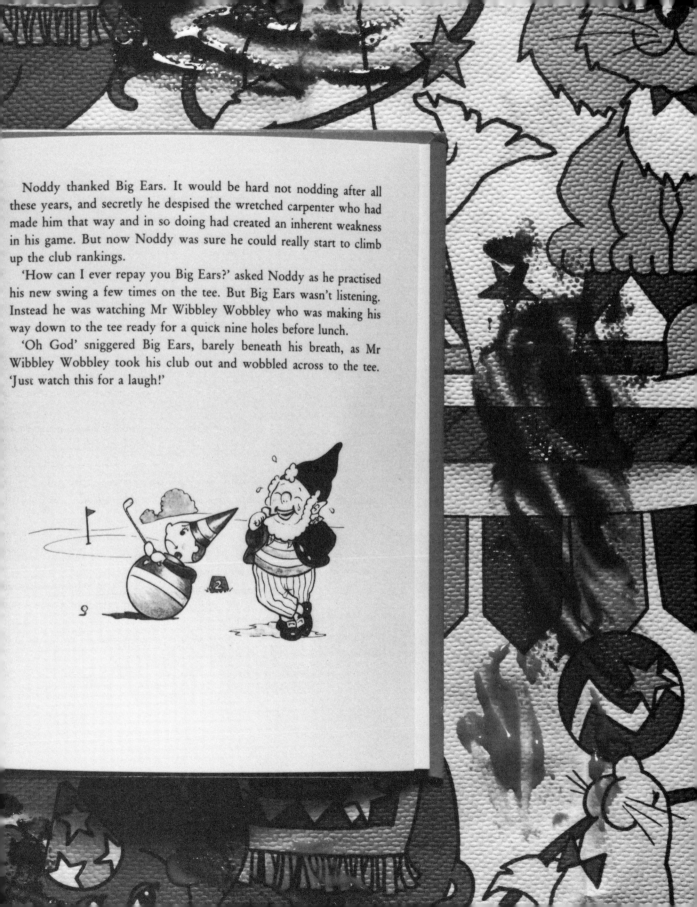

THE THREE BEARS

ONCE upon a time there were three bears who lived together in a house of their own; one of these was called Little Bear, and one was called Mummy Bear, and the other was called Golden Bear. And they each had a full set of irons, and they each had a pro-links golf trolley, and they each had a membership subscription for the local golf club, and they each played off a 10 handicap. And one day, after they had gone out to pick up their copy of *Golfing World*, a little girl called Goldilocks passed by the house and looked in at the window, and seeing nobody in the house she lifted the latch and went in. When she saw three sets of golf clubs she first tried the seven iron of the Golden Bear, but it was too stiff; then she tried the four iron of Mummy Bear, but it was too whippy; then she tried the three iron of Little Bear, and it was just perfect. And then she looked around and saw three golf trolleys in a little line. So she tried the first one belonging to Golden Bear but it was too heavy and she could hardly move it; then she tried the second one belonging to Mummy Bear, but that wasn't quite right either; and then finally she tried the one belonging to Little Bear and it was very easy to control and just what she was looking for. And then, because she was a nosy little sod she decided to go upstairs, where she found a massive wardrobe full of golfing wear. She decided to try on the gear belonging to Golden Bear, but it was really loud and screamed back at her from the mirror and made her look like Coco the Clown on an acid trip. Then she tried the golfing gear of Mummy Bear, but female golfers have never quite got it together fashionwise have they? And, oh God, look at those awful slacks! And then she tried on the golfing gear of Little Bear and it was just what she was looking for, and to cut a long story short, the three bears returned home half an hour later and managed to sell her a matched set of golf clubs, and several golfing pullovers, and a new golfing umbrella, and six pairs of golfing shoes and a new golf trolley (even though she'd bought a brand new one only two weeks ago), and over two thousand pounds' worth of golfing accessories, and . . .

And the moral of the story is: never let yourself get tricked into looking round an empty club shop when the pro isn't there, because you're bound to end up spending a fortune.

—— NURSERY RHYMES ——
FOR GOLFING KIDS

Like any good father you won't want to hang around baby's room singing soppy nursery rhymes and making a complete and utter ass of yourself. However, there is a way to perform this chore and still to profit baby's chances of becoming a top golfer in the future.

Here I reprint a selection from the 'Children's Golfing Nursery Rhyme First Learner'. When faced with bedtime demands, save your blushes by reciting a couple of these golfing adaptations to your youngster.

Doctor Foster
Went to Glo'ster
In a shower of rain
He stepped in a puddle
Right up to his middle
And had to drop out and play
three

Jack Spratt could only drive
His wife could only putt
So between them both, you
see,
They had a lot of trouble in
bunkers

Tweedledum and Tweedledee
Agreed to have a battle
For Tweedledum said
Tweedledee
Deliberately stymied him at
the fourteenth

Round and round the golf
course
Like a Golden Bear
One shot, two shots
Trickling into there★

★ (This contains everything a baby needs to know about golf.
It is also a considerable help in potty training.)

Baa Baa Black Sheep
Have you any golfing
pullovers?
Yes sir
Yes sir
Three hundred different
varieties
In wool, cashmere, and cotton
and acrylic
If you'd just care to step this
way . . .

Barbie Doll golfing widow collection
Burnt dinner
Divorce papers
Golf clubs in trash bin
Changed locks to front door

Pro-Am Care Bears
Knitwear
Trousers
Golfing umbrella
Putting green
Bunker
Pro shop
Clubhouse
Clubhouse bar
Caddie car

My Little Pony 19th hole set
Bar
Tankard
Beer gut
Fat red nose
Double gin and tonic

Mr Men
Mr Overclub
Mr Putting Twitch
Mr Slice
Mr Shank-it

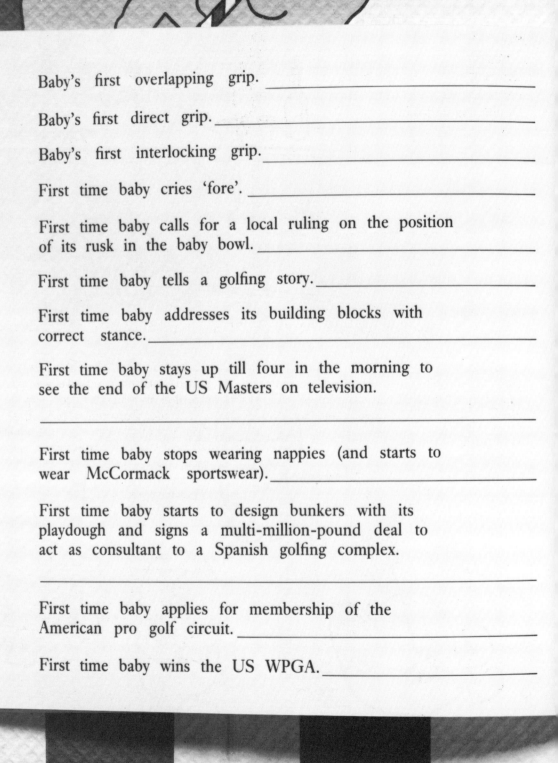

Baby's first overlapping grip. _____

Baby's first direct grip. _____

Baby's first interlocking grip. _____

First time baby cries 'fore'. _____

First time baby calls for a local ruling on the position of its rusk in the baby bowl. _____

First time baby tells a golfing story. _____

First time baby addresses its building blocks with correct stance. _____

First time baby stays up till four in the morning to see the end of the US Masters on television.

_____

First time baby stops wearing nappies (and starts to wear McCormack sportswear). _____

First time baby starts to design bunkers with its playdough and signs a multi-million-pound deal to act as consultant to a Spanish golfing complex.

_____

First time baby applies for membership of the American pro golf circuit. _____

First time baby wins the US WPGA. _____

CHAPTER ELEVEN

GOLFING MEMORABILIA

THE collecting of golf memorabilia has become highly fashionable in recent years and prices paid in auction houses and antique fairs have raced forward at an alarming pace. In a bid to prove that the honest collector can still acquire valuable golfabilia at a reasonable price I have included a small selection from my own personal museum of golf.

—————— FAMOUS GOLFING ARTEFACTS ——————

The Adolf Hitler multi-club
(In 1943 Adolf Hitler received unconfirmed reports that Churchill had taken up golf and was already playing off a nineteen handicap. Furious

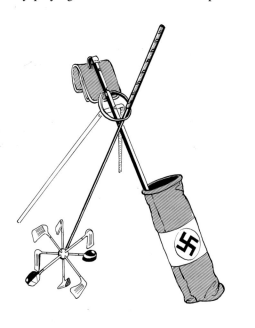

that he was to be left behind, Hitler at once sanctioned work on a massive golf programme and signalled his generals to come up with a golf club that would allow him to play off scratch in four days. The project was eventually aborted two years later with Hitler never having played a stroke. This club, marked with the Krupp Armaments trademark, 1944, has been identified as one of 200 prototypes developed by German scientists working under Hitler's instructions.)
(25p Ipswich jumble sale)

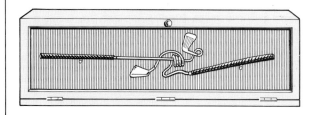

Very rare set of golf clubs from the Uri Geller Pro-Celebrity event
(£1.15 Surbiton car boot sale)

The Turin golfing pullover
(Rumoured to be the golfing pullover worn by the Lord himself.)
(£4.50 Portobello Road street trader)

BUNKEROTOLOGY

The hobby of collecting golfing bunkers has had limited appeal with golfers. The scale of many bunkers, and the difficulty of arranging transportation, have proved the beating of all but the keenest collector. The most ambitious piece of bunker-collecting probably occurred during the redesign of the Championship Course in Tallahassee, when a number of bunkers were to be removed or replaced. A local collector of bunkers announced a plan to remove the most famous sand trap on the eighteenth hole and transport it to his front garden. The elaborate plan involved individually labelling and cataloguing each grain of sand and crating each one separately for transportation. The scheme was eventually abandoned after six weeks' intensive work, during which time less than one square inch of sand had been catalogued.

Two of the most prized and valuable items in my collection are these authentic scorecards, the first from a match between Richard M. Nixon and ex-President Ferdinand Marcos (the signed card shows both players to be at the height of their cheating abilities); and the second from the 1966 Ugandan Matchplay. Arnold Palmer lost but escaped with his life.

	Marcos	Nixon
1		
2		
3		
4		
5		
6		
7		
8		
9		
10		
11		
12		
13		
14		
15		
16		
17		
18		

Match halved

UGANDAN MATCHPLAY FINAL 1966
General Amin v Arnold Palmer

	Amin	Arnold Palmer	
1	5	6	
2	8	9	
3	23	24	(Palmer topped and
4	4	3	holed from 125 yards)
5	7	19	
6	3	4	(89 yd putt given)
7	123	LOST BALL	(later discovered in Amin's pocket)
8	17	18	
9	56	124	(123 off the tee)
10	19	20	
11	2	3	

Amin won 9 and 7

I reproduce here a pair of golfing lithographs depicting famous golfing scenes, picked up for thirty shillings from the Tunbridge Wells branch of the Oxfam Shop (Access and Visa accepted). I estimate that in the 25 years I have owned these lithographs they have increased by at least two shillings in value.

Early hillside art showing prehistoric references to the game of golf

The first battalion of the Queen's Own Golfers going into no-man's land at Ypres, Christmas Day 1916, to play a full eighteen-hole match against the Germans (match halved)

CHAPTER TWELVE

SEXY GOLF

I HAVE been convinced of the enormous sexual potency of the game of golf ever since I read my father's copy of 'Naughty Swedish Nympho Sex Stud Golfer' magazine underneath the bedcovers as a raw ten-year-old.

Since then I have been proved right. Golf *is* sexy. Very sexy. Just look at the men who prove it every day out there on the course: Jack Nicklaus, Ray Floyd, Peter Alliss! And it is this sexual pulling power that gives golfers such an edge over other men, as this prized article by Seve Ballesteros that I keep tucked in my wallet conclusively proves!

'Hello. Seve Ballesteros here.

You know many people, they say me, "Hey Seve, you plenty clever man but why waste all your time playing a sport like golf?" Well let me tell you something, golf he plenty exciting sport okay. But also he plenty sexy too. You'd be plenty surprised how many women golf he turn on! "Hey lady – I'm Severiano Ballesteros, past winner British and American Opens, whose brand of enthusiastic iron play and gutsy unpredictable stroke work around the greens has brought a string of major tournament wins on the professional golf circuit!" No wonder the women they cannot resist such sexy chat-up lines like that. You ask all the girlies. They say, "That Seve, he pretty sexy fella with his natural swing and his uncanny ability to work the ball from the most unlikely of lies, giving him flair and durability, vital components in the tough world of championship golf, where players they play a string of top competitions in a hectic schedule and where fitness, tenacity, temperament and enthusiasm are vital components of the modern golfer's make-up." Hey, what girl she can resist di sexy talk like that?

Yes Mister, this golf he plenty sexy turn on for all di girlies, believe Seve! Take last night. Last night I was in di hotel bar after I finish my round 3, 4, 3, 4, 2, 3, 4, 4, 4, 3, 2, 2, 4, 5, 3, 4, 4, 3 – birdies at di first, fifth, seventh, eleventh, fifteenth and eighteenth, plus an eagle two at the eleventh, producing a round of seven under par, two ahead of my nearest rival, and this despite a stiff headwind for the outward nine, a traditional problem on this most testing of courses where the cut of the greens may cost five strokes on any round. Pretty sexy hot talk hey lady! And as I sit at di bar this lady she lean over and whisper in my ear, "Hello, aren't you Severiano Ballesteros?"

"Yes I am Severiano Ballesteros the talented Andalusian golfer whose raunchy blend of strokes has earned him a place in the annals of golfing history and has brought him such silverware as the Dutch Open, the French Open, the Suntory World Matchplay Championship, the Australian PGA, the Benson and Hedges, the US PGA, and all the top honours in the game!" Well you should just see that girl her face when I lay this sexy golf talk on her. "Would you like to take me upstairs to your hotel room?" she say and listen this girl she is pretty sexy lady.

So I took her up to my room and as she lie there on my bed with no clothes on, pouting her red hot sexy lips, I spent forty minutes going through my scorecard from last year's South African Dunlop Masters explaining how I lost that vital shot on the fourteenth and then I spend another twenty minutes demonstrating revolutionary new putting grip that helped me sink a thirty-five-foot putt on the tricky seventeenth at Fort Augusta.

Yes believe me Mister, golf he plenty sexy sport! Plenty sexy indeed!'

∎

IMPROVING YOUR SEX LIFE THROUGH GOLF

Tips for spicing up your sex life through golf:

1 Do take your golf clubs to bed with you.
2 Do take your golf books to bed with you.
3 Do tell your girlfriend she turns you on as much as looking through the golf equipment adverts in *Golfing Monthly*.
4 Do invite your girlfriend round for supper and when she turns up switch the lights down low, open a bottle of wine and put on a Jack Nicklaus coaching video.

5 Do put your golfing trousers on when your girlfriend suggests you both change into something sexy.
6 Do have your hair cut like Arnold Palmer.
7 Do take your girlfriend to the third round of the Suntory World Matchplay Championships on your first date.
8 Do start telling your girlfriend all about your putting problems in the middle of making love.
9 When your girlfriend asks you to buy her something sexy, buy her a sand iron. If she complains, point out that you happen to find it very sexy even if she doesn't.
10 Don't try to make love to your girlfriend on the back seat of your golf buggy.

THE NAUGHTY GOLF BOOK CLUB

PANEL: 100% MAGENTA + 50% YELLOW

WORDING: REVERSE OUT WHITE

THE JOY OF GOLF
(take in front cover - full colour)

MORE JOY OF GOLF
(take in front cover - full colour)

THE JOY OF PUTTING
(take in front cover - full colour)

THE JOY OF BUNKERS
(take in front cover - full colour)

THE GOLFER'S KAMA SUTRA
(take in front cover - full colour)

LADY CHATTERLEY'S NIBLICK
(take in front cover - full colour)

* RAUNCHY
* STEAMY
* QUITE NAUGHTY

A HISTORY OF EROTIC GOLF
(take in front cover - full colour)

SAND PLAY
(take in front cover - full colour)

FOREPLAY
(take in front cover - full colour)

THE JACK NICKLAUS GUIDE TO BETTER SEX
(take in front cover - full colour)

* CENSORED * BANNED
* TAKEN OFF AT LEAST THREE LOCAL LIBRARY SHELVES

Titles:
- [ ] The Joy of Golf
- [ ] More Joy of Golf
- [ ] The Joy of Putting
- [ ] The Joy of Bunkers
- [ ] The Golfer's Kama Sutra
- [ ] Lady Chatterley's Niblick
- [ ] A History of Erotic Golf
- [ ] Sand Play
- [ ] Foreplay
- [ ] The Jack Nicklaus Guide to Better Sex

ALL TYPE PRINTS SOLID BLACK

● Literature that up till now has not been available in this country.

● The Naughty Golf Book Club includes books that are so sexy they'll have you saying 'Phew, that was a bit sexy.'

To enrol simply fill in the form below:

BACKGROUND PRINT 50% YELLOW + 10% MAG

Name _____

Address _____

_____

Handicap _____

Rules of membership

I agree to take the introductory books at the discount price offered. I realise I must then take a further four books over the next twelve months from the quarterly selection offered. Where more than one book is offered I must take all of them. Where books don't arrive but I receive an invoice I realise I must pay up within seven days or get beaten up by four men in a silver-grey Ford Cortina. Where books arrive that I don't want I may return them within three minutes, providing I still pay over the money. I will not go squealing to Esther Rantzen or any other namby-pamby television do-gooder, and will agree to surrender my chequebook and cheque card to you at any time with a letter of instruction allowing you to draw large sums of money out of my account and deposit them in a private Swiss bank account. Where a lorryload of books arrives unannounced at two in the morning I will agree to buy them all at twice the marked publisher's price, in cash, no questions asked, schtum, schtum, or I will never see my wife or children or kneecaps again. I realise I can cancel this agreement at any time only on pain of death (and a £5000 cancellation fee).

THE FACTS OF LIFE FOR GOLFERS' KIDS

When a man and a woman love each other very much, then it is only right that they want to share this love together, and the most natural way that they can share their love for each other is by the woman allowing the man to go off and play golf all day Saturday and Sunday and never mind the shopping and the housework and those odd jobs around the house.

Left: This rough layout for a forthcoming magazine advertisement has just come into my possession . . .

'Sexy, Sinful and Seventeen Over Par' – the first golfing blue movie

THE FREUDIAN INTERPRETATION OF GOLFING DREAMS

Many golfers experience vivid dreams. Some of these dreams are common, and their interpretation has been studied and documented.

NUDITY

The player finds he is on the tee and is completely naked. He asks his caddie for a three wood, and the caddie produces a large German sausage that he waves about in the air.

Interpretation: This dream is motivated by fear. The player is afraid of being made a fool of on the golf course. He is afraid of being exposed. Hence the nudity. The German sausage is a phallic symbol. It has no part in the actual dream but helps to make the dream more interesting and always gets a good laugh.

TUNNELS

The player finds himself wandering down a long tunnel when a voice calls 'fore' and an enormous golf ball flies towards him.

Interpretation: In this dream the tunnel represents a tunnel and the large golf ball represents a very large golf ball. In effect it reflects the player's terror of wandering down a tunnel and being hit by a very large golf ball. Which is pretty unlikely and therefore a very silly dream to have had in the first place.

WATER

In this dream the player finds he is drowning. Every time he calls out for help a man appears and throws him a sand iron.

Interpretation: This dream reflects the golfer's fear of the water hazards. Whatever he does he still ends up in the water. He feels trapped. The sand iron probably comes from a completely different dream and shows that the dreamer is suffering from interference in his dreams and is picking up more than one station.

FALLING

The player finds himself falling in an empty void with only a set of knitted heads for his golf clubs to save him. He tries to make these into a parachute but fails and ends up as a double-glazing salesman in West Wickham.

Interpretation: This shows a player's great desire to return to the warmth of his mother's womb. In effect the player has failed to come to terms with his golf and wants to start again from scratch. The knitted heads to the golf clubs almost certainly represent the Pope, or the male sex organ, or a type of rare Andalusian fruitbat, or something else entirely different. The double glazing is a complete red herring and just goes to show you can't believe everything you see in dreams.

SEX

A stunning model invites the golfer to go to bed with her. He does and they make mad passionate love several times, including the one where she pretends to be a schoolgirl.

Interpretation: Who cares about an interpretation??? What are you, mad? You have a dream like that and you want to wake up and ask what it means!!!

CHAPTER THIRTEEN

GOLF AND THE ARTS

ANYONE who has seen the preliminary sketches for the Venus de Milo 'Chipping out from 40 yards at the Fourteenth', or heard Debussy's 'Serenade to the Lofted Mashie' knows the enormous inspiration offered by golf to the artist. Few of us realise that Wordsworth was in fact playing a quick eighteen holes on the Borrowbeck Course when he first wrote those immortal words:

I wandered lonely as a cloud
That floats on high o'er vales and hills,
When all at once I saw a crowd,
A host, of golden daffodils

How strange it is to consider that had he not hooked his tee shot so far to the left then he probably never would have seen those daffodils. Out of adversity was born such a wonderful poem, and what a lesson is there for all of us Sunday golfers. The next time we badly connect with a shot we should think first before complaining, in case the words that come out are a stream of wondrous poetry.

And the same is true of Beethoven. It is often forgotten that Beethoven's symphonies were named after golf holes. Beethoven's First, Second, Third, and so forth all took the names of golf holes, the Eroica dog-leg par 4 being perhaps the best known. It is sobering to think what might have happened had he continued to compose for longer than he did, for very soon he would have been faced with the predicament of what to name his works.

If he had been a member of the full eighteen-hole golf club, who knows what extra pleasure we might have enjoyed from the deaf old German golfer. Beethoven's Ninth is indeed an Ode to Joy, whoever she may be. But what would Beethoven's Eighteenth or even his Nineteenth have been like – an Ode to Orgasmic Ecstasy perhaps?

In the world of the theatre, playwrights have long drawn on the immortal game for inspiration. Chekhov's 'Cherry Orchard' was originally entitled 'Dog-leg around the Cherry Orchard and a Short Iron to the Green'. How many of us know that?

Shakespeare's 'Anthony and Cleopatra' was at first entitled 'Anthony and Cleopatra versus Bobby Locke and Arthur Hagan in a Matchplay Fourball' – a remarkable piece of foresight predicting the emergence of the two great golfers three centuries before they were to thrust through to prominence. And in an early manuscript of 'Hamlet' it is quite clear that the most famous speech in all the Bard's works was written as 'two wood or not two wood, that is the question'. The word 'wood' was replaced by the word 'be' only at the very last minute, and no doubt after a great deal of soul-searching. Indeed, there are still many scholars who question the change from 'wood' and feel that it destroys the essential integrity of the speech. (See, for instance: Denton & Marks, *Shakespearean Plays, Their Intention & Meaning: A Golfer's Approach*, University of Fort Augusta, 1979; Leibsick Troome & Hardicot, *The Interpretation of the Works of William Shakespeare:*

an ontological study with special reference to the world of the professional golfer, The Bob Hope Pro-Am College, 1983; and MacTaggle & Crombie, *Shakespeare, Golfer or Playwright*, Edinburgh University Press, 1948.)

And in opera too we can clearly see the influence of golf. The parting scene in 'The Marriage of Figaro' originally took place on the seventeenth green at Royal Birkdale – a hitherto little-known fact that radically alters the whole complexion of the piece and reveals a far stronger golfing theme than was originally supposed. Indeed, even 'Swan Lake' originally contained a scene in which a passing golfer attempts to drive over the lake with a four iron, narrowly missing the swan and stymying his opponent on the green. In some versions, this scene was retained till quite recently and was dropped only when the golfer started to take a longer ovation at the end than the principal performers.

The truth is that golf has been an inspiration to the arts for centuries, and in deference to that debt I now include a number of examples of this happy liaison. I begin with a piece by Oscar Wilde. Written with great perception in 1906, when announced it caused an even greater storm than Wilde's later homosexual relationships and it was never published. I now take the opportunity to print it here for the first time. It is perhaps difficult for us today to appreciate the scandal it must once have caused.

Roger Snelgrove and Cecilia Grimsby during the world première of their production of 'The Importance of Being Earnest'. (Director: Arnold Palmer)

THE IMPORTANCE OF BEING EARNEST

Adapted for the stage by
Lee Trevino & Ben Crenshaw

Additional dialogue by
Tony Jacklin

Morning room at Lady Bracknell's house in Argyle Street. The room is well appointed. A large window looks out onto the garden. Jeavons is arranging afternoon tea on a table whilst Lady Bracknell sews. A golf ball whistles through the open window and lands at her feet. It is followed by a knock at the door.

LADY BRACKNELL: Who on earth can that be at this time of day?

Jeavons returns from the door

JEAVONS: It is the Golden Bear, the great Jack Nicklaus, ma'am.

LADY BRACKNELL: Show him in Jeavons.

Jack Nicklaus enters with his caddie

JACK NICKLAUS: Lady Bracknell.

LADY BRACKNELL: Jack, what brings you this way?

JACK NICKLAUS: My short pitch and run to the green at the eighteenth ran through, leaving me an awkward chip to the flag if I am to retain the parity with the course.

He points to his ball on the carpet

Lady Bracknell inspects it through her glasses

LADY BRACKNELL: Sit down Jack.

JACK NICKLAUS: Thank you Lady Bracknell. I prefer to stand.

LADY BRACKNELL: Then you will afford me the courtesy of listening to what I might have to say from where you stand. I may address you freely I trust?

JACK NICKLAUS: Of course Lady Bracknell.

Lady Bracknell approaches closely as a good golf-coach might do when instructing a pupil

LADY BRACKNELL: Jack, you are addressing the ball too squarely. Do not be afraid to work the clubface – hit cleanly through the line of the ball, rolling your wrists for extra lift.

As she speaks a second ball comes through the window and lands at her feet

LADY BRACKNELL: What is that?

JEAVONS: A golf ball ma'am.

LADY BRACKNELL: A golf ball! To mishit one tee shot through the green may be regarded as a misfortune; to mishit two looks like carelessness.

There is a knock at the door. Jeavons departs to answer it while Lady Bracknell demonstrates the flat point in Jack's swing

JEAVONS: The great Gary Player, ma'am.

LADY BRACKNELL: What, the great Gary Player, three times winner of the British Open, twice winner of the American PGA, a tough and gritty South African who has been on the pro circuit over thirty years and who in his time has won all four major titles?

JEAVONS: He didn't say, ma'am.

LADY BRACKNELL: Show him in Jeavons.

Jeavons shows Gary Player in. He wears his traditional all-black gear. He is accompanied by his caddie who tows behind him a large golf trolley

LADY BRACKNELL: Mr Player.

GARY PLAYER: Lady Bracknell, I will not burden you with my misfortune. I allowed my wrist to roll over when chipping a simple wedge through the green and in through your window.

LADY BRACKNELL: Mr Player, I have long admired your blend of plucky iron play combined with elegant stroke work that has made you a regular money earner of the pro circuit. Would you perhaps do me the honour of showing me your swing?

He steps forward and demonstrates

LADY BRACKNELL: Try not to straighten your left leg. Remember, true power comes through good leg action. When I'm playing

2

badly I concentrate on my legs and upper body. Here, like this. See how I allow my body to swing freely with a light easy grip. You have a try.

Gary Player takes the club from Lady Bracknell and tries to loosen up. As he does so Jeavons enters from behind

JEAVONS: Tea, ma'am?

As he approaches Gary Player draws his club back and sends the tea tray flying

LADY BRACKNELL: Kindly do not intrude Jeavons. I am instructing Mr Player in the use of the iron.

There is a further knock at the door

JEAVONS: Mr Severiano Ballesteros ma'am, a Spanish golfer, he wishes to play through.

JACK NICKLAUS: Seve's cavalier brand of approach work often forces him into unpredictable lies others would find unplayable.

LADY BRACKNELL: Please Mr Nicklaus I will handle this. Jeavons, you attend to Mr Nicklaus and Mr Player while I address the lanky Catalonian heartthrob who has done much to put European golf back on the map.

JEAVONS: Yes ma'am.

Enter Severiano Ballesteros

LADY BRACKNELL: Seve.

SEVE: Lady Bracknell, I felt I should come at once and show you my new grip.

END OF ACT 1

GOLF AT THE CINEMA

The cinema owes no less a debt to golf. Principal among the pictures I remember are those listed below, culled from the pages of *Halliwell's Golfing Cinema Yearbook* for 1985.

Sam Peckinpah's *Highlights of the 1981 British Open at Carnousti*
When Jack Nicklaus plays his final approach shot to the eighteenth green in the 1981 Open at Carnousti he receives an ice-pick through his head. A frank and often bloody film, it offers a sensationally brutal look at the world of professional golf. The scene where Tom Watson is hacked to death by his own seven iron is particularly memorable, offering a savage indictment of the American pro-am circuit.

A Kind of Putting, 1961
A young North Country golf professional is forced into marriage, has to live with his dragon-like mother-in-law, and finally comes to terms with a flat swing that causes him to quit on his tee shots and hook them violently to the left. A blunt melodrama with a strong golfing message that was seen as a milestone of its time.
(Alan Bates, Thora Hird, Bert Palmer, Gwen Nelson, Gary Player)

The US PGA Version of *Apocalypse Now*, 1984
A Vietnamese golf professional is instructed to give a golfing lesson to a club player who has retired to the hills and is closing his clubface too much on his follow through and pulling his drive as a result. Some vivid scenes along the way, especially when the club player's double bogey on the ninth puts him under pressure and eventually sees him going down three and four in the first round of the Saigon City Matchplay, but often the film seems to lose its way and blurs its message. Marlon Brando, as a caddie, turns in a workmanlike cameo performance, but under the joint direction of Francis Ford Coppola and Lee Trevino the film seems strangely unsure of its viewpoint.
(Martin Sheen, Robert Duvall, Marlon Brando, Sandy Lyle, Sam Torrance, Bernard Gallagher [as himself], and Nick Faldo as a merciless Viet Cong war veteran)

Psycho 4 (384 yards, stroke 12), 1985
Alfred Hitchcock's deft reworking of his own *Psycho* movie, especially adapted for a golfing audience. The story is simple but effective. Norman Bates has been released and the Bates' motel has reopened with the first guests being a group of club golfers on a weekend golfing holiday. During a tense and climactic ninety minutes the motel owner (played by Sam Snead) recalls some of the great shots of his illustrious career and recollects fifty years of the American golfing scene.
(Sam Snead, Bobby Jones, Roberto de Vicenzo, Bob Charles and Shelley Winters [as the bunker])

Tony Jacklin's *Exodus*, 1970
The early years of the state of Israel, as seen through the eyes of Tony Jacklin (past British and US Open champion).
Heavy-going modern epic, based loosely on Tony Jacklin's *Play Better Golf*. The parts depicting the birth of Israel

tend to be weak and insubstantial, but the sequence dealing with the short ball game around the green is regarded by many as a classic. Filmed entirely on location at the Southern Hills GC in Oklahoma.
(Paul Newman, Lee J. Cobb, Peter Lawford, Ralph Richardson, Peggy Mount [as Arnold Palmer] and the 1969 British Ryder Cup squad [as the people of Israel])

Black Emmanuelle on the Kings Course, St Andrews, 1978

First of the series of soft porn movies starring Sylvia Kristel and Peter Alliss. The bored bride of the French consul to Scotland is initiated by Peter Alliss into various forms of sexual activity. The fact that neither partner ever removes any clothing but that instead they discuss golfing statistics for the entire ninety minutes left many critics mystified, but golf fans loved the soft-focus mix of golf's favourite commentator and a sexy model, and the film spawned a number of sequels: *Emmanuelle Plays Winter Rules at Turnbury; Emmanuelle Goes Three Over Par During the Second Day of the US Masters; Emmanuelle Moves up Six Places on the US PGA Tour; Emmanuelle Makes up a Fourball with Jack Nicklaus, Severiano Ballesteros and Tom Weiskopf.*

Two Iron over the River Kwai, 1956

British POWs in Burma are employed by the Japs to build a new eighteen-hole golf course; meanwhile, British agents seek to destroy it. Ironic adventure epic with many fine moments but too many centres of interest and an unforgivably confusing climax in which a dispute over local rules causes the Japanese guards to open fire. The film is distinguished by Guinness' portrait of the English CO who initially decides to set his sand traps short of the green at the seventeenth, but finally changes his mind and in an emotional scene admits to his men that the course would have been better had they been placed ten yards further down the fairway ready to catch wayward approach shots.
(Alec Guinness, Jack Hawkins, William Holden, Henry Longhurst and introducing Sonny Rawlings as Archie)

The Summers of Winter, 1964

Made by the respected Russian director Pastanov Bogobogovitch, the film tells the tale of three peasant families forced to move to Moscow and their conflicting attempts both to come to terms with their new circumstances and to take up the game of golf. The film is often regarded as Pastanov's most ambitious work, lasting a full twenty-eight hours and telling as it does the entire story of the Russian Revolution as seen through the eyes of aspiring golfers. It was originally denounced by the Kremlin as subversive, but has since been forgiven and now enjoys an important position in the Russian film archives.

GOLF AND DANCE

It is almost as though the visual interpretation of golf was made for the dancer. The evidence is everywhere to be seen: the constant references to golf in *West Side Story*, the immense influence of golf in the work of Busby Berkeley, and of course the almost fanatical devotion to golf seen in the work of Andrew Lloyd Webber. Anyone who has seen *Phantom of the Opera* and has not been struck by the enormous similarity between the work and play on the back nine at Royal Lytham in the third round of the 1958 British Open, must have had their eyes closed. Equally, the musical *Evita* surely draws its inspiration from the 1930 Walker Cup at Royal St George's in which Bobby Jones beat Roger Wethered 9 and 8 and preserved his 100 per cent record in his fifth and last single, while Donald K. Moe held the most remarkable score standing 7 down with 13 to play but winning with a birdie on the last for a final round 67. The likeness between the theme to the musical and the events on the golf course is quite remarkable.

None the less, with space at a premium I have restricted my selection to just two pieces which between them seem to sum up the bond between dance and golf.

THE 'GARY PLAYER IN THE SAND TRAP, CAN HE GET OUT IN PAR?'

First of the true golf dance crazes to sweep America. Dance to an up-tempo rhythm. Your partner stands to one side holding an imaginary set of clubs.

Dai Rees and Edmundo Ross had a hit with 'La Bunka' because of its close association with the 'Gary Player in the sand trap, can he get out in par?'

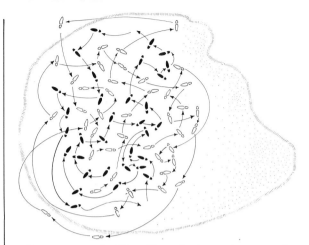

Dance steps to the 'Gary Player in the sand trap, can he get out in par?'

A complicated movement from the same routine

THE SANDY LYLE TWO-STEP

1 Player stands with toes pointed outward and with weight somewhat back on his heels and equally divided between both feet. Bend slightly at waist to prevent tenseness. The girl turns the left side of her body slightly away from the man.

2 As body winds up, the shoulders, arms, hands and club follow. Clubhead starts low along the ground and follows the body turn. The girl shifts her torso to the right side, placing weight on the right foot.

3 The man keeps his head steady all through the swing. His left arm continues to be straight as possible without a feeling of stiffness. The girl turns the right side of her body slightly away from the man. The girl's left hand stays upon his shoulder. Don't over-exaggerate your hip movements so that you bounce up and down on the dance floor and top the ball.

⸺GOLF TO MUSIC⸺

Greg Norman performing his highly elaborate 'dying swan' golf swing

Andrew Lloyd Webber attends rehearsals for his new musical 'Song & Dance & Golf'

Recording of 'Everybody's Doing the Golf-a-ling-a-long'. (Golfing songs were a popular craze in the late 1920s. Particular favourites were 'Coochie Coochie Coochie Coo, May I please Play Through-oo-oo'; 'The Golf Bag Rag'; 'the Two Iron Jitterbug', and 'Can I Clear the Bunker Can Can')

FINE ART

And finally to golf in the world of art itself. Here we are spoilt for choice, so often have the two been linked.

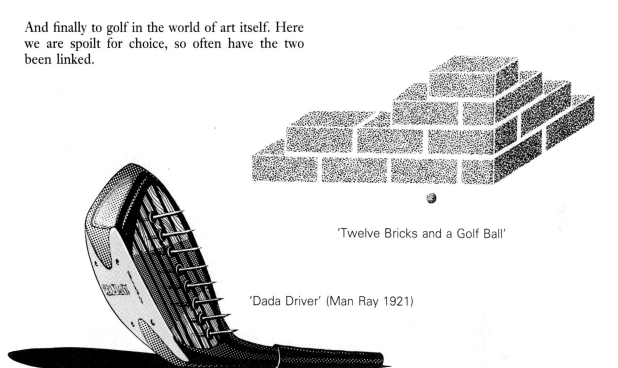

'Twelve Bricks and a Golf Ball'

'Dada Driver' (Man Ray 1921)

'Hole in One'
(Lichtenstein
1962)

I HELD MY BREATH AS THE TINY SPHERE REACHED THE DISTANT NADIR OF ITS ARC...

THOKK!

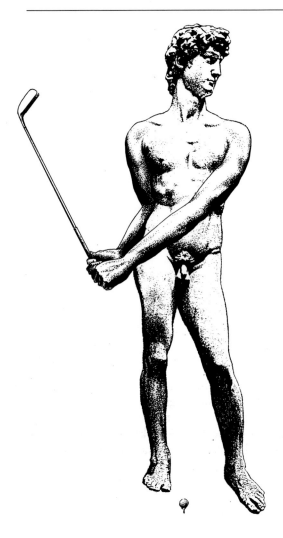

Above: 'The Boy David' (Michelangelo 1504)

Above right: 'A Difficult Lie by a Jar of Sunflowers' (Van Gogh 1878)

'Madonna with Matching Set of Woods' (Raphael 1517)

CHAPTER FOURTEEN
RELIGION AND GOLF

THAT some believe golf to be a religion is often plain. I myself do not hold with this view. However, a novel and interesting theory is that religion is golf. This radical standpoint has been proposed by the American golfing theologian Aaron P. Offenhausen, in a working paper 'The Bible and Golf' in which he proposes several novel theses.

In this paper he attempts to draw examples from the world of religion to indicate how the message of golf is told through the word of the Lord, and in addition he seeks to extemporise on the theme by offering new examples of the biblical story of golf.

It is a view that after consideration I personally cannot support, but it does bear investigation and for that reason I summarise below the more salient points from Offenhausen's work.

(The following pages are extracted from *The Bible of Golf*, University of Fort Augusta Press, 1985.)

Left: *Vincent Fernandez summons up all his powers of concentration to raise his sand iron successfully by meditation*

The chipping the green to within two feet o
the flag
(The Gospel according to Fuzzy Zoeller)

In this chapter Simon is having problems with his short b
game. He asks Our Lord what he should do. Jesus tells h
to cast out the stiffness from his swing and play throu
cleanly and naturally. Simon experiments with the adv
and finds that very soon he is able to close down his clubf
and improve his accuracy to within a few feet of the fl
Simon asks what he must do to repay the advice. Simo
love is enough, says our Saviour, but a G & T wouldn't
amiss squire.

The laying on of hands
(Oosterhuis Chapter 7, verse 13, par 4)

The Lord is walking in the market place when He
approached by a man who tells Him he has a terri
problem with his putter and cannot control a twitch that
causing him to miss the hole by three or four feet. The Lo
lays His hands on the putter and says 'Behold, your putti
problem is healed.' The man goes away and immediat
wins the All Ishmail County Classic. In this parable the Lo
demonstrates the strength of His love by showing how
can cure even the worst putting problem.

The Ten Commandments
(Tarbuck, Chapter 7, verse 12, 385 yards)

In this chapter Jimmy Tarbuck attempts to rework the T
Commandments to give more understanding to the golf
The text begins: 'Thou shalt not covet thy neighbou
putter. Nor his two handicap. Nor his matched set
graphite clubs . . .'

8

The Miracles
(Tom Watson, Chapter 18, 418 yards, par 4)

Jesus is walking the Bethlehem West Course, measuring out the holes, when He sees a water hazard ahead. A man runs up to Him and explains his ball has landed in the water. Jesus tells him to kneel at His feet and close his eyes, and when he opens them again the water has gone and his ball is a simple seven iron to the green. The man thanks Jesus and asks Him if He can do something about the bunker to the left of the green on the thirteenth.

The pullover of many colours
(Graham Marsh of the Apostles)

Joseph is marked out as his father's favourite son by the gift of a special golfing pullover of many colours. Joseph's brothers are jealous of the gift and vow to kill Joseph. But they change their minds at the last minute and decide instead to shrink the pullover so that it is too small for Joseph to wear.

The testing of Job

God tests Job by sending down mighty suffering upon him. He loses his favourite mashie and develops an acute putting twitch. He finds he is quitting on his swing and suddenly develops a nasty slice. He doubles his handicap in six months. His short iron play goes to pieces and his golfing trolley loses a wheel. Finally, he pulls a tee shot up against a tree stump and the rebound nearly blinds him.

Job cannot understand how God can allow him to suffer like this. He questions God and asks Him why He persecutes him so. God responds to Job's challenge by revealing unto him power and wisdom and by giving him some useful tips on underclubbing. Job realises at last that God is bigger than him, and he has his faith restored.

In the light of Offenhausen's work a number of golfers got together to rewrite the Bible in terms of the golfer, as a way of showing that the golfer has a fundamental role in the Church. I recently was lent a copy of this book for the purposes of review. Below is a selection from my edited notes. I leave the reader to judge for himself the worth of the text.

The parting of the waves

In the Bible we learn how Moses leads his people into Israel by parting the waters of the Red Sea. Clearly, God is trying to tell us that when we face a similar problem we should take our courage in both hands, open our shoulders, and drive forth over the water. Some contend that God is in effect encouraging us to gamble. I disagree. He is simply saying that provided we have confidence in our swing and do not underclub, then there is no reason why the presence of water should have any psychological effect on our shot.

The casting out into the wilderness

Jesus is cast out into the wilderness for forty days and forty nights. (And when He returns He announces He has completely changed His grip and is now playing a two wood off the tee on a 350 par 4, although this later piece of information is unstated in most versions of the Bible.) In effect, we are being told that we may need to spend time practising to improve our game. In this instance God chooses the wilderness as His example; we might quite equally replace that with the practice green or the practice hole.

CHAPTER FIFTEEN

WHO'S WHO ON THE GOLF COURSE

M Y OWN personal photo biography of golf folk.

'Ratty' Wiggins, the human ferret. It is claimed that there has not been a ball lost that Ratty hasn't been able to retrieve. The trick lies in the scent. Before the round Ratty rubs his nose in your balls. Should your ball then be lost, Ratty simply follows the smell. Here we see him burrowing six feet underground to retrieve a ball that inadvertently went down a particularly extensive rabbit warren.

The SAS Caddie Division. For a small charge you can hire a fully trained SAS officer to act as your caddie. As well as normal caddie duties the officer will show you how to snare a fox and build your own survival hut. In addition he will help you disarm your opponent and take him prisoner, plus he will show you how to storm the club bar using stun grenades and a 2.2 mortar, and help to provide vital ground support should you wish to launch an air attack on the handicap committee. For full details contact The British Army, c/o Flat 10A, 47 Neasden High Road, London NW10

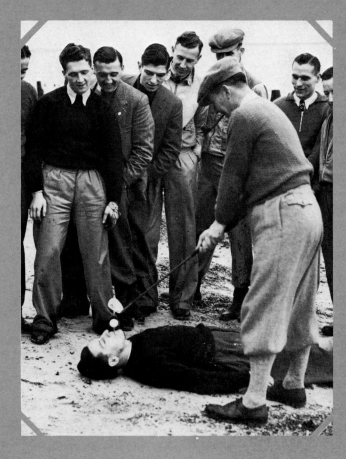

Above left: Melissa Davidson, the first human tee. Faced with appalling unemployment in her native East Fife, Melissa applied for and received a government small-business grant to set herself up as a human tee. The advantages over conventional tees are considerable. The human tee can respond to minute instructions from the player, and of course there is far less chance of actually losing a tee like Melissa. Unfortunately the need to tunnel her way beneath the tee, along with a series of crippling hand injuries, forced her to close down her business after just twenty minutes

Above right: Donald Peacock. Following Melissa's lead a number of other enterprising youngsters saw openings for themselves. Donald was perhaps the most successful. In addition to his 'mouth tee' (seen here) he could also tee a ball up on the end of his toe, and following the example of Pétomaine, the French flatulator, he could even support a ball above his buttocks for several seconds, ample time for a player to line up his address and drive

Left: The man from the Fourteenth. Terry Collett spent many years in full-time employment as an itinerant ball collector. A former Olympic swimming champion, Terry, who sank to this futile and pathetic existence, is rightly credited with originating the Government's job creation scheme

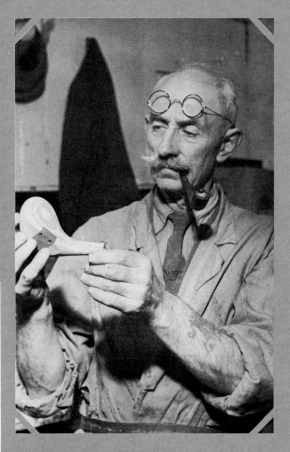

Above left: Cad U R. The most unusual in a new line in animal-
powered caddie cars. Here we see the donkey-powered version.
Other animals have proved equally endearing, although early
experiments with a brace of white rhinos on a course at Weybridge
have been less than satisfactory

Above right: Rex Norbertson, club maker. Rex was one of the
last breed of club makers. He worked entirely without tools
or tackle, using only his bare teeth to nibble away a giant piece
of wood to its final shape. Weeks of painstaking work went into
every club, and yet try as they might they couldn't persuade Rex to
change his diehard ways. Known as 'Nibbler' Norbertson (or 'Norbert
Nibblerson), he claimed the work actually improved his teeth by
giving them strength. Others claimed he was a complete loony who
hadn't been the full shilling since the day he was born

Below: The band of the Dragoon Guards plays out the final holes
in a display of massed golfing by the men of the Queen's Own
Golfing Regiment. Precision golf drill marching was popular
between the wars, and despite the inconvenience many players
insisted on playing only with a full regiment in support

CHAPTER SIXTEEN

GOLFING FICTION

THAT many golfers turn out to be able writers is clearly seen. One need only look at the great array of golfing books large and small by both past and present players to see the literary word lurking beneath many a golfing swing.

But what is perhaps less well known is the number of straight writers who have at one time or another turned their hand to golf.

I append three examples that to me show how broadly the influence of golf has spread. Doubtless many others could be added.

RUPERT BROOKE

Struck the church clock at ten to three
And is my golf ball on the tee
And will the flag appear to move
Just as I swing with arms held smooth

And causing me one shoulder raise
And catch the ball a passing graze
And cuff it lightly o'er the top
That sends it in a five-foot hop

And would my shoulder ligaments tear
And cause me to scream and swear
And kick my foot and stub my toe
And make it start to throb and glow

And would I say you little tit
And boot it forward in a fit
And when my partner did protest
Would I say shut your gob you pest

And would I vengefully destroy
All the equipment at my employ
The marker box, the bench, the tee
And go upon a vengeful spree

And when I'd fully spent my ire
Would I calm down and say 'right squire
That is enough of practising
Now let's get on with the real thing'.

1
ESCAPE FROM STALAGLUFT 48

The Colonel eyed the men suspiciously, then spoke in a low voice for fear he might be overheard.

"At ease men." His manner was composed, a steady ring to his voice. Half a dozen of his fellow officers sat around the room whilst outside others kept watch should a goon appear.

"Bad news I'm afraid," he confessed when he at last assured himself that all was secure. "Ridgeley and Popperwell were caught trying to go over the wall. Luckily neither of them was shot, but the Commandant has insisted they be moved to a more secure prison."

There was a sigh as all the men present drew breath. They had felt sure that this attempt would succeed and put an end to the miserable sequence of failures that had overtaken their every escape plan: 84 escapes undertaken, 84 escapes failed. It seemed as though they would never beat their duck, never climb from the foot of the POW Escape League table where they now languished.

Bottom Six:

Camp	Attempted	Won	Lost
Stalagluft 17	12	1	11
Stalagluft 42	34	1	33
Stalagluft 34	56	1	55
Colditz 'B'	1	–	1
Bremen Reserves	72	–	72
Stalagluft 48	84	–	84

ESCAPE FROM STALAGLUFT 48
(Extract by kind permission)

As they sat rueing their failures a bright voice called out from the rear of the room.

"Permission to speak Colonel." The voice was keen and eager. It had a freshness now lost in the older men.

"Go ahead Perkins."

"Well sir, I know this probably sounds a bit of a gamble sir – but – well, I have a plan that I feel sure will work."

There seemed little enthusiasm in the room. They had been over every possible plan. Retreading old steps. There wasn't a new plan to be had. The Colonel sniffed disdainfully.

"Very well Perkins," he spoke without looking at the man. "Let's hear it."

"Well sir," Perkins paused, the audacity of his idea still surprising even him, "well before the war I shot quite a decent round of golf . . ." A barely stifled groan ran round the small room.

"Get on with it Perkins!"

"Well sir, I thought – well, if I pretended to be a golfer, a *French* golfer, and I claimed I had hit my tee shot astray and was simply looking for my ball . . ." The Colonel sucked through his teeth for a full five minutes before pursing his lips to speak.

"Let me get this straight Perkins," he spoke in a deep and sincere voice. "You are proposing to go up to the guards, pretending to be a French golfer whose ball has strayed off course and inadvertently landed in an English prisoner-of-war camp?" Perkins nodded.

"And how d'you explain the fact that we are 250 miles from the French border?"

"I have a problem with my drive and I'm inclined to hook." It was indeed an audacious plan. No tunnel. No climbing. Surely it would never come off, and yet – what had they to lose? A string of failures longer than a gypsy's curse.

"What do you need?" The Colonel spoke without excitement.

"A golfing jumper, and trousers. And a full set of matched clubs. Preferably French. And a ball. Oh, and a trolley would be useful."

"A trolley?" A note of petulance rose in the Colonel's voice.

"If I am to do this thing at all then it is to be done properly."

"A trolley," sighed the Colonel, and wrote the words down with a suck of his pencil. The others in the room seemed unsure. The plan was surely doomed to failure, and yet . . .? They couldn't help holding a small measure of grudging admiration for the young airman's plan.

12

"What about documents?" The Colonel was now warming to the plan, it seemed.

"A scorecard for the Paris Metropolitan Golf Club, with local rules. A membership tag for the same course. A directory of French golf strokes. My last medal card. A list of the rules of golf. In French. And a complete set of French golf coaching manuals."

Arranging for copies to be obtained for forging wasn't easy. True, they had tame guards who could obtain many local items, but full documentation for a French golfer? None the less they were soon ready and Perkins ably equipped for the role ahead.

Six weeks of frantic French cramming had enabled him to pick up the rudiments of French grammar, and it was decided the escape plan should not wait a minute longer. All that now remained was for the guile and ingenuity of Perkins' plan to reap its reward.

Outside the guards were about to change. Perkins knew those going off duty would be keen to be away and less likely to be inquisitive. And sensing his moment he tossed his ball into the sandy expanse of no-man's land between the trip-wire and the fence before striding boldly after it.

The response was swift and immediate as the rattle of machine-gun fire cracked through the air and the sound of angry voices raised the hue and cry.

"Was is das!!!!????" The guard pointed at Perkins' ball, lying as it did ten feet from the fence.

"Was is das!!!????????" The guard shouted again as Perkins failed to reply.

"Bonjour Monsieur," Perkins offered his hand in greeting. "Je suis Pierre Papillon, un golfer, je regrette je suis un peu off course et ma balle est arrivée là, dans votre camp."

The guards stared at him nonplussed as he stood there, golf club in hands, sizing up his lie.

"It iz not possible!" the guards seemed unconvinced of his argument.

"Mais oui, j'agree," Perkins replied without hesitation, "c'est plus impossible cette lie."

"Not ein lie!" growled the soldier. Perkins hesitated for a minute.

"Ma carde." He spoke confidently as he handed his scorecard to the officer. The soldier surveyed it for a few seconds.

"Why are you 350 kilometres off die course?" he snapped angrily.

"C'est mon grippe," replied Perkins apologetically, swinging his

13

club through the air to illustrate his problem. "Tout le temps je suis hooké à la gauche."

The guard resurveyed the card then handed it to his colleague who stood there, machine-gun finger twitching, reading it carefully. There followed a pause while they discussed the matter. All his papers were in order, and it was true he did have a quite appalling grip that would seem to render a hook shot almost an inevitability. And they were off duty in little more than five minutes. At last they seemed to relax slightly.

"Very well Herr Golfer, you must play through."

This was it: Perkins' chance. Freedom lay an enviable short step away. He paused. He drew back his club, addressed the ball, and he smacked it sweetly at the fences. There was a pause as the fence took the strain then set the ball flying in the direction of the first guard's nose. He whimpered with a strangled cry as blood poured freely from the open wound.

Perkins composed himself and drove quickly at the ball again, this time topping it viciously and sending it into a near impossible lie at the foot of the fence. Three shots later he had only driven the ball further to ground.

The guards, despairing of their charge, stepped forward. Perkins tensed. Had they suspected? He felt a bead of sweat run across his brow, then a cold gnawing terror as they snatched the club from his hands.

"Nicht, nicht, nicht!" they screamed at him, "Not like das, like dis!" And they pointed at the open gate.

"Drop out on the other side of the fence and play two!" And with that they frogmarched him to the outside world.

Five minutes later he was clear. Clear of the camp. Clear of the guards. And just 750 short miles from Blighty. If he could just keep his head down and avoid rolling his wrists too much he might be there in less than six months. He paused, drew back the club and swung with all his might.

Two minutes later there was a knock at the camp gates. The guard who opened it took in the sight before him. It appeared to be a golfer.

"Bonjour," smiled Perkins as pleasantly as he could, "je regrette mais mon balle has just landed inside votre camp et je wondered if je might fetchez la?" '

14

Escape from Stalagluft 48 *Lance-Bombadier Perkins tries out a possible disguise as a French maiden under the watchful gaze of the Colonel*

AGATHA CHRISTIE

(From: *The Oxford Companion to Golfing Literature*)

Wrote seldom on the subject of golf, although over her lifetime drew from her patchy knowledge of the game spasmodically. Perhaps the best known of her golfing novels was *The Sand Trap!*, in which a lost golf ball holds the clue to a murder. The piece was not a success but it did provide her with the plotline for *The Mousetrap*, although in this later piece all references to golf were expunged from the text.

She flirted with golf again in a brief playlet entitled *The Golfing Murders*, a tedious and predictable work in which a series of murders takes place in a golf clubhouse. The story is not helped by the author's sketchy knowledge of the game – she constantly refers to 'the golfer removing his swing from the boot of his car', and 'the ball landing in the silly sandy thing instead of on the nice green lawny bit with a flagpole in it'. Indeed, at one point the author even refers to one of the golfers striding up to the tee and bowling a left-arm inswinger down the court. It is a weak piece that has not surprisingly never been produced professionally, and its failure no doubt accounts for Miss Christie's refusal to return to golf as a theme for nearly 25 years, although there are those who claim that *Death on the Nile* was prepared under the working title *Death on the Ninth*, and the draft of *Ten Little Niggers* was by some accounts conceived under the name *Par Ten Little Niggers*, the word 'par' being dropped only when it was discovered to have absolutely no relevance whatsoever to the piece, besides being possibly ever so slightly racist.

In an early Miss Marple story there is a chapter in which that lady wins the 1952 Southern States Classic and goes on to score a creditable 281 (72–69–75–65) in the US Seniors Invitation Event at Heritage Village, Wisconsin, including a forty-foot chip to the flag at the eighteenth and a remarkable eagle on the 41-yard par 5 sixth, claiming a total of $4321 prize money for the series (showing that the author had learnt from her earlier mistakes and was now much more *au fait* with the golfing world), but again it is not one of the author's better pieces.

A flirtation with golf in *Murder on the 9.14 to Carshalton Beeches* (which briefly passes the Reigate golf course, though not actually stated as such in the text) is the author's last dalliance with the world of golf, although in her autobiography she refers to her regret at never having been invited to take part in *A Round with Alliss*, a loss not unconnected with the fact that she died twenty years before the programme was first recorded.

CHAPTER SEVENTEEN

GOLFING TIPS

Slow play

Slow play is a constant frustration on many courses, but there's no need for you to resign yourself to the problem.

Treat the players ahead as an obstacle to be cleared, in much the way one might attempt to drive a bunker. Do not shout a warning.

Having played your shot, walk casually down the fairway thanking them warmly for having had the courtesy to wave you through. Should they deny having made such an offer you should immediately become defensive. Tell them you could have sworn this was their intention and regret that such a misunderstanding should have taken place, pointing out that there was never any desire on your part to send a golf ball screaming within three inches of their unprotected heads.

On no account surrender your advantage or agree to play behind.

I have long been an advocate of learning to play golf through newspaper strips. These are particularly suited to those players whose idea of a really good read is confined to assessing the slope of a green. Here are a few of the strips published under my name with my caricature. (Well, Jack Nicklaus's didn't look like him, did they!)

HOLDING THE FLAG AT THE WRONG ANGLE

Many players lose the chance to score strokes against their opponent when holding the flag for them.

Holding the flag upright allows a player to gauge the lie of any putt accurately.

Try standing at an angle to imply a gradient — like this.

Your opponent will naturally read a 'borrow' that isn't there and will miss the hole by several feet.

USE OF THE CLUB BAG

Here is a useful trick to assist with difficult chip shots. With your opponent's attention diverted elsewhere place his club bag on the green directly behind the flag.

You can now overhit any shot confident that the bag will break the pitch and may even secure a useful rebound into the hole.

Your opponent is left with two options; concede the hole completely because of the interference of his bag or allow your shot to stand. *Either way you cannot lose.*

The use of beavers at water hazards

When a ball lands in a water trap, too many players elect to drop out and lose strokes where a little prudent forethought might help.

Always carry round a pack of beavers in your golf bag. When your ball hits a water hazard you should release the beavers into the water upstream of the ball. Six months later they will have erected a beaver dam, halting the water flow and drying out the downstream river-bed sufficiently for you to take up your stance.

You are now free to play your stroke unhindered and may collect your beavers and proceed with the round without losing a shot.

THE TRICK GOLF BALL

If your opponent is playing particularly well it may be necessary to take desperate measures. One of the most desperate, and most efficient is through the *wrist-breaker tee*. When your opponent tees up divert his attention momentarily and replace his ball and tee with the one shown. It looks like the conventional set-up but in this case the ball and tee are made from a single piece of tungsten steel, strengthened to withstand a force of 97G. The tee itself is 8" long and incorporates a screw shaft which will not move even under the force of the most powerful drive. The result is dramatic for, as your opponent strikes his ball, the effect is to block his stroke stone dead.

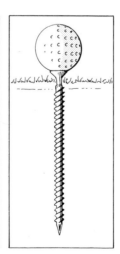

Few players can continue their round after such an 'accident' and must retire immediately to bathe their wrists and recover from the shock. Deny any knowledge of the bogus tee when asked.

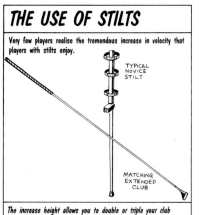

THE USE OF STILTS

Very few players realise the tremendous increase in velocity that players with stilts enjoy.

TYPICAL NOVICE STILT

MATCHING EXTENDED CLUB

The increase height allows you to double or triple your club length and with this comes an attendant increase in the power of ones stroke.

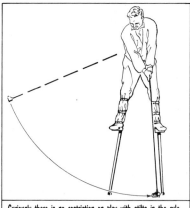

Curiously there is no restriction on play with stilts in the rule book and players on stilts can regularly drive five or six hundred yards.

Do beware low or overhanging trees or overhead cables. Many 'stilted' players forget this elementary precaution with devastating effect.

Beating the nerves on the first tee

Everyone knows the terror that can grip the novice golfer on the first tee. Combat these nerves by diverting attention away from your golf towards something else.

Try wearing something outrageous, such as the front half of a pantomime horse. Or emit a loud baaing noise from the moment you leave the club-house, punctuating it with a series of high-pitched squeaks and whoops.

Or try wearing a pair of exploding waterproofs that ignite in a ball of flame the moment you address the ball.

All of these will distract the gallery's attention and allow you to play your shot in a relaxed frame of mind.

TREADING YOUR OPPONENT'S BALL INTO THE GROUND

Players encountering their opponents ball first can usually enhance their chance of winning by treading the ball into the ground.

Just remember the three golden rules:
1. Don't attempt to tread on the ball while your opponent is actually playing it.

2. Restrict your sabotage to one quick tread. Do not attempt to accompany yourself on the yukelele in an elaborate five minute 'clog dance' on top of the offending ball.

3. Do not be over ambitious and use a pneumatic drill or industrial digger to increase the size of the cavity.

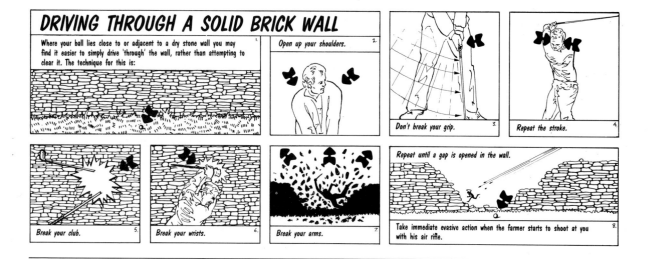

DRIVING THROUGH A SOLID BRICK WALL

Where your ball lies close to or adjacent to a dry stone wall you may find it easier to simply drive 'through' the wall, rather than attempting to clear it. The technique for this is:

1.

Open up your shoulders. 2.

Don't break your grip. 3.

Repeat the stroke. 4.

Break your club. 5.

Break your wrists. 6.

Break your arms. 7.

Repeat until a gap is opened in the wall.

Take immediate evasive action when the farmer starts to shoot at you with his air rifle. 8.

Getting out of bunkers the complete cheat's way

Bunkers cause golfers some of their worst frustration. Here's a tip to take the sting out of them.

Approach the ball as normal and take up your address. On your back swing release a pressurized sand canister concealed in the toe of your golf shoe. The pre-set explosive charge inside the canister should coincide with the downswing of your stroke and will shower you in a mini sandstorm for up to five seconds.

During this time you can pick up your ball and carefully throw it on to the green, emerging seconds later covered head to toe in sand and remarking absent-mindedly that you will need to talk to the pro about the excessive sand you seem to take with your sand irons.

Put on a great show of mock surprise on noticing your ball two inches from the flag (actually, if you can throw it that close you might consider taking up bowls – or at any rate boules).

Confusing your opponent's line on the green

A ridiculously easy trick to master, and still surprisingly effective.

Make a point of 'walking the line of the green' before your opponent makes his putt. Try to exaggerate this walk to the extreme: drag one leg, hobble, affect a false gradient, make a great play of an invisible ridge; roll and sway like a man on a circus rollercoaster. The combined effect is to put your opponent so off his swing that he finds it quite impossible to line up his shot.

Mountaineering gear and crampons are definitely over the top.

CHAPTER EIGHTEEN

THE GOLFING BOOK OF RECORDS

ARID statistics or records tell us little of the game. They are invariably dry and bare and give little indication of the true excitement of golf. And yet occasionally they can throw light on the subject.

The records I list below have been culled from my own extensive collection of golfing annals. I hope you gain as much insight into the game through reading them as their compilation has given me.

GOLFING FACTS AND FIGURES

THE WORLD'S SHORTEST HOLE

This is to be found at the fifteenth tee of the New Course, Baffin Island. The hole measures approximately 5 ft 6¾ inches from tee to hole (4 ft 2½ inches from the women's tee). The hole is unremarkable in its construction, a simple three-foot fairway, diminutive two-foot-square green, and no hazards or rough to speak of, the only impediment being a miniature bunker to the left of the green. The hole was constructed in the knowledge that Baffin Island was hardly the most accessible location, unless you are a penguin, and was quite deliberately designed to attract a passing trade from the club golfer who sought at least one hole in one in his lifetime. For a while it served its purpose, intrepid golfers travelling several thousand miles simply to gain that all-important hole in one. Nowadays the hole has been superseded by 'Hole in One World' in Connecticut, a remarkable eighteen-hole course in which none of the holes measures more than sixteen inches. The result is that players may amass an entire round of 'holes in one' without the need to travel.

MOST INCLINED GREEN

The seventeenth at the Plato del Grosso course in Panama offers the world's steepest green. The green is maintained at a perfect ninety degrees. Opinion varies as to the reason for this strange feature, although it is more than likely the result of Spanish conquistadors invading the region in the fifteenth century and attempting to subvert the local Aztec leaders by encouraging them to build golf courses that were totally unplayable and which would hence bring derision upon them every time they attempted to play. The seventeenth is the only known example of such a hole still in use today. A memorial at the foot of the green lists the names of the two hundred green-keepers who have lost their lives attempting to cut new holes on the green.

RUDEST CADDIE

Undoubtedly this dubious honour goes to Sagemore Tuffit, a West Country caddie who was known to have 'the foulest tongue in all of Somerset'. Even before a ball had been played he would have rudely denounced the player, his family and his family's family in a torrent of slanderous abuse. And all this after simply being asked what club the hole played. He would then go on to accuse the player's wife of being a black Jezebel, and the player himself of being the product of wedlock between a donkey and a cabbage. Throughout the round, Sagemore would continue his vitriolic diatribe, swearing and cursing and accusing the player of every sin under the sun. If asked the distance to the green, he would reply by announcing that if the player could not judge something as simple as that then he needed his head submerged in a bucket of fresh cow dung and his manhood massaged with a steel boathook. Enquire of him the borrow of the green and he would simply snort like a camel and call you the most ignorant small-brained fornicator this side of the moon. During an attempt at a tricky shot to the green he would stand cat-whistling and waving two fingers beneath your chin, and should you in fact get the right line and weight on a putt he would ensure it missed by drawing the flag from the hole and using it to smack the ball away, explaining that anyone of your sub-cretinous brain size simply didn't deserve to hole such a putt.

After a while it became quite fashionable to be partnered on your round by Sagemore, and he drew a quite enviable following as players flocked to become the butt of his fiery tongue. Indeed, such was the demand for his services that some players would refuse to turn out unless they had Sagemore at their side, heaping scorn on their game and their private lives. At last the pressure began to tell, and Sagemore started to run out of things to say and would simply spend the entire round blowing raspberries whenever his player was playing, and when addressed for any reason would simply resort to screaming 'pink blancmange' at the top of his voice before attacking the nearest player with an ice-pick. He eventually retired from the world of golf and was last heard of working for British Gas.

WORST EVER LIE

Many players lay claim to this honour, but amongst the most worthy must be Lionel Barrowclough's predicament at the eighth at the Royal Course, Umbatabetse, in the Congo Basin. Having driven a loose wood from the tee he was alarmed to discover his ball had lodged in the open jaw of a sleeping crocodile. Anxious not to drop out and lose a shot he elected to play the ball as it lay, and drew a four iron from his bag. Securing a reasonable stance on the river bank, his feet astride the animal's mouth, he opened up his shoulders and let swing a mighty shot at the crocodile's jaw. Unfortunately, at this very moment the animal chose to stir, and lowering its jaw was surprised to find a golf club suddenly embedding itself into its chin. The crocodile, alarmed at the violent searing pain filling its jawbone, reacted quickly, leaping at Barrowclough as he tried to make his escape up the river bank. The crocodile snapped away ferociously as Barrowclough beat it about the head with his long iron. Thankfully he kept his cool, and his grip, and was able to land a series of well-aimed drives on the creature's snout. The battle seemed to last an hour or more but eventually the greater guile of Barrowclough held out, and with a final groan the animal rolled over on its back, the life drained out of it, its jaw falling open to reveal the ball still lodged firmly in its gullet. Seizing his opportunity, Barrowclough took the now twisted iron and with a clean swing drove the ball some 120 yards, clear of danger.

(Some years later, debate still continued about whether Barrowclough should have lost a shot for this incident. He had after all addressed the ball as it rested in the animal's mouth and had swung his club intending to hit the ball. Indeed, there were those who maintained that the several hundred blows to the creature's head that Barrowclough had employed to release his ball equally constituted strokes. In the event the rules committee suggested no penalty be lost on either account, but that two strokes be added for time-wasting.)

MOST DANGEROUS GOLFER

Colonel Oliver P. Huggett, the Australian player, is generally acknowledged as the world's most dangerous player. At the last count eight people had been killed and a further sixty injured by his efforts around the course. The Colonel's great problems stem from his rubber-shafted driver designed exclusively to the Colonel's own specification. The club, while offering the extreme whippiness demanded by its owner, was clearly unpredictable in its behaviour and quite liable to send a shot in any of 360 degrees. Moreover, the extreme springiness of the club meant that the Colonel had to develop a cast-iron grip to hold on in the face of the great momentum built up by such a swing. This grip took the form of an elaborate strapping combined with a length of steel wire used to bind the club to the Colonel's hands. The result was successful in its intent, ensuring the grip didn't break during the stroke, but the outcome was to transfer the great energy of the rubber cue to the Colonel, who would invariably fly several feet through the air at the end of his downswing, propelled by his own latent muscular energy. Many were the people injured by the great weight of the Colonel landing on top of them as they stood well back on the tee, while at least three incidents of heart attack seem to have occurred in unsuspecting bystanders witnessing the Colonel's erratic behaviour. Curiously, the Colonel himself seems to have escaped relatively unscathed from his exploits.

SLOWEST ROUND OF GOLF

The record must go to a fourball match playing the nine-hole North Pole Course in the heart of the Arctic Circle in 1963. The match started on 1 June of that year and wasn't completed until 8 December 1965. The fact that the course is laid out on an unstable ice floe which can cast players adrift from their balls for months on end did not help. Nor did the use of white balls on the frozen landscape, which often meant a search of several days to find them again in the icy wasteland. Finally, the onset of the Arctic winter with permanent darkness and temperatures as much as sixty degrees below meant that for six months of each year no strokes could be played and the players had to hole up in their base camp waiting for the skies to clear.

HOLES IN ONE: MOST AT ANY HOLE

One.

(There are very many instances of a player hitting a hole in one. But despite the extensive chronicles of the game there is no record of any player ever securing two holes in one at the same hole at the same time. The nearest any player came to achieving this occurred at a Canadian club event in 1972 when Hogie Graham hit a six-iron shot to the flag at the fourth. The ball hit his partner's ball on the green, knocked it in, and then rolled in itself. Unfortunately it was foggy at the time and there were no other witnesses, but Hogie himself was quite adamant that the chain of events did occur as he told them, despite having only that morning been released from gaol for a series of hoaxes and frauds.)

GREATEST EVER CHEAT

In an uncharted field it is naturally difficult to be certain of any contender's qualifications. However, the achievements of Wilmot Deakins constitute a record that few of us would hope to match. His greatest cheat was a round of seven on his local course, showing a card on which for five successive holes he didn't even record a shot, claiming the ball had bounced from one cup to another.

FUNNIEST GOLFING ANECDOTE

The funniest golfing anecdote was first told at a golfing dinner in Surrey in 1957. The piece was so funny that the following day eight people were still laughing, two seriously. The item itself involved the club professional's wife, a new member to the club, and the local vicar. The anecdote was prepared by the golf anecdote writing team of Barnaby, Dribble & McCoy who together prepared over 13,000 golfing stories and anecdotes from 1951 to 1967, and published several books on the subject including *Anecdotes for Golfers*, *More Anecdotes for Golfers*, *Even More Anecdotes for Golfers*, and *Anecdotes for Golfers, the Complete Works*. The team won the coveted Golden Rose in the world-famous Golfing Anecdote Writers Awards at Royal Birkdale in 1969, narrowly beating entries from Albania, Bulgaria and Ecuador.

(Note: *Esquita los Andros 'Out of Bounds'*, written by Señor Jose Philipos, was published posthumously in 1986 and contains over four hundred pages of Ecuadorean golfing anecdotes, including 'The Mixed Threeball and the Alpaca', and 'The Llama in the Clubhouse'.)

MOST FASTIDIOUS GREENKEEPER

Conrad Broom, the legendary South African greenkeeper, is accredited as the world's most fastidious greenkeeper. Players on his course are prohibited from going on any green without written permission. Shoes must be removed and feet thoroughly washed beforehand. Club rules allow compulsory deportation for any player disobeying these rules, and persistent offenders are shot. Conrad's dedication to the art is astonishing. He uses a micrometer to measure the height of the grass and will spend days cropping the surface with a pair of manicure scissors. Conrad waters every inch individually by pipette, while every slice of grass removed during cutting is sent away by Conrad for autopsy.

MOST FORGETFUL GREENKEEPER

Ivor Hughes, greenkeeper at the Cardigan Bay course, Abertyffi. Ivor is so forgetful that he regularly forgets where he has left his greens, and spends many hours wandering round the course looking for them. Indeed, so forgetful is he that on occasions he has forgotten he is a greenkeeper altogether and has gone to work in fishmonger's overalls. Over the years his forgetfulness has steadily increased. He regularly forgets which green is which and places the flags in entirely the wrong position, causing the players to play a quite different game of golf from the day before. Or sometimes he forgets how many holes there are and simply places all the flags on the same green.

STERNEST CLUBHOUSE RULES

The Munich Golf Club of 1937 is regarded as having had the strictest rules of any golf club. The club committee, under the guidance of the Waffen SS, undertook a purge of previous members and in their place installed a zealous right-wing dictatorship. Among the rules introduced were:

- Saluting fellow players
- All caddies to goose-step
- Moustaches to be worn at all times
- Albert Speer to redesign the new clubhouse
- Half-track golf caddie cars to be introduced
- The Club pro shop to be re-armed.
- The committee to invade Poland and annex the Sudetenland

LEAST WELL-EQUIPPED CLUB SHOP

Belongs to the Mosckva Golf Club, at the exclusive one-hole Lenin Course. (Eighteen holes is a Western decadence, brought on by imperialist greed.) During the last visit by Western golfing correspondents in 1987, the shop had just two golf clubs and one golf ball on show. The first club was the Riga, made from solid cast iron and measuring some ten feet tall; it weighed approximately three hundred pounds and was produced by the massive Riga Golf Club Manufacturers and Sheet Steel Rolling Mill in Doentsk. The second club was the Ivanitch 2000 Club-pro, a graphite steel club with a contoured vulcanised grip. Unfortunately the factory making the club head will not produce anything for at least another five years, and for the time being the shaft is being sold on its own. The golf ball for sale was the Leningrad Matchplay Super, of which a total of three are made annually. The balls cost just over 750,000 roubles each, with taxes (or £95,000).

THE TALLEST TEE EVER EMPLOYED

The tall tee competition run in 1948 was an effort by the Golf Tee Manufacturers Board of the USA to excite more interest in their product. Golf tee manufacturers have always been aware of the low social esteem and poor self-image of their product. After all, the golf tee is the last thing most people think of when watching a golf match. This was an attempt to redress the balance by showing that tees could be fun. In this context was launched the first ten-foot tee, or 'Big Ten' as she became known – a giant of a tee, fashioned in the normal style but with a full ten feet between ball and ground. The only way players could reach the ball was by stretching upwards on tiptoes and knocking the ball off the tee with a nudge from the club. For a short while tall tees became fashionable for their novelty value, but no lasting change emerged and tees soon returned to their normal height.

The new 'bigger' ball proved unsuccessful as the rule makers failed to pass a new 'bigger' hole

THE ROUNDEST BALL EVER USED
The roundness of the ball is a feature few players tend to comment upon. However, in New Zealand a few years ago a craze for 'round-balling' took over and players would bet large sums of money as to whose ball was the roundest. Special 'Round-Ball Testers' were manufactured to measure the roundness of balls to a very high level of accuracy, and thousands of pounds changed hands in wagers. Unfortunately it was soon discovered that all balls were as round as each other, which rather spoilt the betting. In 1874 the Laird of Pitlochry travelled to London to tell Parliament that he had discovered a ball so round it was rounder than even the roundest ball he had ever set eyes on before. He was promptly thrown in an asylum and was never heard of again. Until now, that is.

WORLD'S MOST EXPENSIVE BUNKER
To be found on the exclusive Bel Air Golf Course in Beverley Hills. Everything on the course has been designed to better anything available elsewhere. And nowhere is this more apparent than in the case of the special theme bunkers. The first boasts genuine Saharan sand, authentic camels, and a full Bedouin encampment. The second has a mosque, oil well, and a sign welcoming you to Saudi Arabia. The third is decked out with cacti, wild buffalo and a full mock-up of the OK Corral. And so forth. Mishitting your tee shot is the gateway to an event, rather than a disaster.

WORLD'S LARGEST GOLF TROLLEY
The 'Great Bird' was the brainchild of Howard Hughes. Convinced that his path to immortality lay in creating the world's largest-ever golfing trolley, Hughes spent fortunes to put together this vast vehicle. Over forty feet high, and with a wheelbase of over twelve yards, the caddie kart was impossible to navigate round a golf course. Indeed, the only place it could move around was on a specially converted airfield in the Nevada desert. After several years and millions of pounds in development, Hughes eventually abandoned

the scheme with the kart never having been used, and devoted his energies to a scheme to introduce underwater ping-pong and a device to repeel a banana skin once the banana had been eaten.

WORLD'S MOST INFORMED CADDIE

Josiah MacGovern, caddie on the Edinburgh & Peebles course between 1972 and 1981. Few who went round with him could doubt his extraordinary powers. Asked to calculate the distance to the green he would offer a figure without hesitation, invariably proving accurate to within two or three inches. He could detect wind speed to within one knot with his nose, predict the line of a putt from 200 yards away without looking, and would have a player's club ready three shots before it was required.

He was in addition brilliantly informed on matters of the day and could hold a conversation with four people at the same time, each one more erudite than the next. He was an expert on political theory, an eminent historian, a scientist of international repute, a wit, raconteur, showman, and could recite the entire works of William Shakespeare from memory. So well read and respected was he that players felt guilty asking him to carry their clubs and would very often hold them themselves, leaving Josiah free to expound and theorise.

He eventually retired from the game in disgrace at the age of seventy-two when he misjudged the distance to the pin by an enormous six feet and became so mortified with grief he felt unable to go on.

APPENDICES

BOOKLIST

The author would like to acknowledge the following texts that were invaluable in the preparation of this book.

A Shorter History of Japanese Golf Courses, USAF Bomber Command, 1945.

Putting the Linda Lusardi Way, Sexy Book Publications, London, 1987

The Reader's Digest Illustrated Book of the Golf Tee, Reader's Digest, 1982

A La Recherche Du Golfe Perdu, Jean-Paul Sartre, 1959

Little Red Hook, Mao Tse-Tung, 1954

Invasion of the Death Ray Zombie Golfers from the Planet X, Pulp Press, New Jersey, 1962

Les Picton: The First Golfer Megastar, Liar Books, London, 1978

Country Diary of an Edwardian Golfer, Milkit Books, 1983

What to Name Your Baby, (2000 names, each with a golfing connection), Bolton University Press, 1969

The Time-Life Encyclopaedia of Sods, (the world's first reference book devoted entirely to the divot and sod), Time-Life, 1986

GOLFING ASSOCIATIONS

Those wishing to pursue particular interests in golf may wish to make contact with one of the more specialist bodies that have been set up to cater for minority golfing interests, the principal among them being the following:

- The Unprofessional Golfers' Union
- Federation of Cheating Golfers
- The Transvestite Greenkeepers' Association
- The Kamikaze Caddie Club of Japan
- The Pro-Islamic Death to Imperialism Sons of Martyrdom Fundamentalist Golfing Circle
- The Confederation of Breakdancing Club Stewards
- The Surrey and District Sisters of the Revolution Golfing Association
- The Federation of Stunt Golfers
- The Anglo-Tibetan Golfing Exchange
- The European Sub-Aqua Golfing Society

———— DICTIONARY OF GOLFING TERMS ————

Terms used in this book are defined thus:

Address: That which a golfer fails to give when driving his ball through a set of plate-glass windows overlooking the course.

Back door: Any shot which takes a pirouette before entering the hole and which is normally claimed as intentional by a club player.

Birdie: A hole that is completed in 1 under par. Thus, in the case of a par 4 hole, a birdie is obtained when a player holes out in 3 lucky shots as opposed to 4 lucky shots.

Blast: General form of verbal address given after playing a sand shot.

Bolt a putt: When a putt is struck so hard it causes structural damage to the hole as it sinks.

Borrow: What a player generally does when asked to stand a round in the clubhouse.

Cut shot: Name given to any badly-sliced shot that accidentally leaves the ball in a half-decent lie.

Divot: Form of sod removed from the course by inexperienced player, as opposed to the green-keeper, who is another form of sod that many would wish to remove from the course.

Dog-leg: Hole in which the rank amateur is compelled by unnatural forces beyond his control to play in a straight line, in contrast to straight holes that he is compelled to play as dog-legs.

Dormie: That point at which a losing player decides that it should not be the result that matters but rather the act of playing, and upon this basis suggests that all bets should be recalled and the game played out purely for fun.

Eagle: A hole in which a player uses up his year's quota of fluke shots in one go.

Fairway: That which a player playing six on a long hole is heard to answer when asked how far it is to the flag.

Gimme: A putt claimed when the ball lies within thirty feet of the apron.

Grasscutter: The golfing equivalent of an Exocet; takes on the properties of a two-hundred-foot putt.

Halved: A hole is halved when both players discover they have cheated equally.

Hazard: Anything at all within a quarter of a mile of the tee that impedes progress.

Lie: That in which the club golfer can compete on equal terms with the professional.

Lost ball: Mysterious ball that having been lost for 15 minutes suddenly discovers itself on the lip of the green.

Press: To attempt to hit a ball three times farther than one has ever hit a golf ball before.

Rough: Area of grass which is considered an artificial obstruction from which a player can drop out.

Rub of the green: That which is deemed ill luck when adversely affecting one's own ball, and unfair luck when profiting an opponent.

Shank: That by which one may secure a hole in one on holes adjacent to the one you are at present playing.

Sky: Any ball that would secure a hole in one were the hole to be on a plateau 200 feet directly above one's head.

Stance: The position in which one stands immediately before clubbing an innocent tee to death.

Tee: That which a player blames for everything when he misses his drive on the first hole.

Windmill: A swing in which a player attempts to demonstrate the workings of the piston aero engine.

Woods: Where most players go in search of their balls.

CORRECT SCORING ——NAMES FOR HOLES——

The avian designation of scoring shots at a hole has recently been extended to include the following fuller titles.

PAR

3 UNDER	Albatross
2 UNDER	Eagle
1 UNDER	Birdie

PAR

1 OVER	(Bogey) Peewit
2 OVER	Moorhen
3 OVER	Cormorant
4 OVER	Shag
5 OVER	Canada goose
6 OVER	Crossbill chaffinch
7 OVER	Roast chicken
8 OVER	Common or North American gannet
9 OVER	Blue-crested peahen
10 OVER	Joey the budgie
11 OVER	South American macaw
12 OVER	Tufted reed warbler
13 OVER	A tit
14 OVER	A real tit
15 OVER	Red-throated diver
16 OVER	Wagtail meadow pipit
17 OVER	Mountain linnet
18 OVER	Stormy petrel
19 OVER	Lesser spotted grebe
20 OVER	Woodpigeon

THE GOLFING PYRAMID ————LETTER————

There have been pyramid letters before; but none like this. This pyramid is built on the misadvice every amateur golfer rushes to offer his fellow player. By following the instructions we could effectively increase the total national net handicap by 1,345,987 overnight. And all that for the price of just six stamps.

Start by copying out the letter opposite six times, inserting the relevant information in the missing sections. Point out to the recipients that in return for your valuable advice he or she should now address six similar letters to his or her friends offering equally useful help.

[address]

Dear [name]

    For several weeks I have been watching your game and have noticed that you have a [insert description of problem here] I hope you won't mind me pointing this out because I too suffered with a similar problem several years ago, but was luckily able to cure it quite easily by [insert the description of the cure] I'm sure if you took the same steps you too would be amazed at the improvement in your game. I know I was.

    There is no charge for this service but you are asked instead if you would send <u>six</u> copies of this letter to fellow golfers, inserting the relevant problem and advice as appropriate.

    In this way every golfer in Britain will have received a free golfing tip for the price of just six second-class stamps.

    This pyramid depends on your co-operation. Your failure to take part could cost several thousand golfers their handicap.

    Best wishes

[your name]

—————— GOLFING ADVICE FOR EMERGENCIES ——————

Lightning

Lie the victim flat on the ground and keep him calm. On no account loaf around snorting 'that was a bit of a lark', or shout out ' 'ere, what d'you do for an encore?' On no account tell him not to move because you want to take a photo for the kiddies, or remark that the poor victim looks better without his hair and anyway it didn't seem to do that Michael Jackson any harm.

Bee sting

Rush the bee to hospital immediately. Take the sting with you. Try to reassure the bee and keep it warm.

Snake bite

Remember, it is possible to suck out snake venom if you get to it early enough. Be suspicious of any unmarried male players with seafaring friends who claim to hold extra-sensory powers of prediction and offer to suck out the venom from your personal regions before you are bitten.

Love bite

Start to wear polo-necked jumpers. (For love bite by snake, tell the snake beforehand quite firmly that you don't wish to know.)

Nuclear war

Wherever possible play should continue. If a nuclear warhead lands within 4 miles of your lie you should check local rules on nuclear fireballs.

Invasion by Martian space army

Play winter rules.

Photographic Acknowledgements

The photograph of the author on page 12 was taken by Raymond Thatcher at La Quinta Club, La Manga; those on pages 12 (left-hand column), 15 (top right and bottom), 16 (bottom), 17 (all three photographs), 36, 87, 98 (top left and top right) and 101 are from Associated Sports Photography.

All others are by courtesy of the Photo Source.

The photograph of the famous golfer with Seve Ballesteros on the back of the jacket is by Robert Bluffield.